THE *MYSTERY* OF CONSCIOUSNESS

Donald E. Mansell

Pacific Press Publishing Association
Boise, Idaho
Oshawa, Ontario, Canada

Edited by Lincoln Steed
Designed by Tim Larson
Cover by Michel Tcherevkoff/Image Bank ©
Type set in 10/12 Century Schoolbook

The author assumes full responsibility for the accuracy of all quotations cited in this book.

Library of Congress Catalog Card Number: 87-72908

ISBN 0-8163-0742-3

88 89 90 91 92 · 5 4 3 2 1

Dedicated To

my grandchildren
Donnie, Erika, Elizabeth, Charlie, and Monica

Contents

"We shall try our best to do as you say," said Crito, "but how shall we bury you?"
"Any way that you like," replied Socrates, "that is, if you can catch me and I don't slip through your fingers."

—Plato in *Phaedo*

Chapter 1

Soul-Survival

Out-of-Body Experience

Nineteen-year-old David Whitaker remembers the crash of metal on metal as the speeding Chevrolet Impala caved in the left side of his car. Then everything seemed to go blank. The next thing he remembers was hearing a terrible buzzing sound and feeling as if he were passing rapidly through a dark tunnel. After emerging into what seemed like bright sunlight he had the sensation of floating in the air near the wreckage and seeing himself slumped over the steering wheel of his demolished '86 Mustang.

As he watched in stunned disbelief, he could see passersby running toward the wrecked cars. Then he heard Karen screaming, and saw his girlfriend exit from the passenger side of the car, crying hysterically but apparently uninjured.

It all seemed unreal as David saw an ambulance screech to a halt, sirens wailing, and watched the paramedics carefully extricate his seriously injured body through the passenger door. After checking his pulse one of them muttered, "He's dead."

"So is this what it feels like to be dead?" wondered David. Looking around in bewilderment, he noticed diaphanous figures floating toward him as if in slow motion—his sister June, who died two years before of leukemia, and his Aunt Mary, who succumbed to a heart attack when he was a boy.

7

Other familiar figures were beginning to come into focus. Just then David heard one of the paramedics say, "Let's give him CPR anyway." Immediately the men began applying cardio-pulmonary resuscitation.

All of a sudden David heard that terrible buzzing sound and again felt himself whooshing through the dark tunnel. Next he remembers feeling excruciating pain on his left side and seeing the faces of the paramedics bending over him—then blessed unconsciousness. When he awoke he found himself in the intensive-care unit of the local hospital in critical condition but alive.

Fiction? No, say researchers, just a typical case of a person who has had an out-of-body experience (OOBE or simply OBE) and lived to tell about it.[1] Many who have gone through an experience such as David's are convinced beyond a shadow of doubt that in OBEs the soul temporarily leaves the body and returns.

After examining data on hundreds of similar cases, some researchers as well as others are convinced that personal consciousness survives death as an invisible entity popularly called the soul or spirit.

But OBEs are not the only strange phenomena that have persuaded millions that the dead are alive and conscious—and that they sometimes communicate with the living. Many who have never had an OBE insist that the soul or spirit survives death because they have actually *seen* their dead loved ones. Here is an example.

Apparitions

Some years ago when I lived in Paradise, California, I became acquainted with a couple by the name of Bill and Helen Schmidt. One day they told me about a strange experience they had recently had.

Francis, Helen's eldest son by a former marriage, had recently lost his life while racing in the Indianapolis 500. His mother was watching the race on TV and witnessed the horrible pileup. The shock of hearing the announcement that her son had been killed was almost too much for her.

That night Helen couldn't sleep. Outside the moon was shining, its bright beams flooding her bedroom. As she lay awake crying, she hoped that somehow the terrible tragedy hadn't really happened.

Suddenly she heard familiar footfalls. Getting up, she went to the window and looked out. She couldn't believe what she saw. To her utter astonishment there was Frannie coming up the sidewalk toward her! There could be no mistake about it. She was wide awake. She pinched herself to make sure. This was no dream. It *was* her son!

Helen's heart skipped a beat as he approached. He passed so close to the window she could have reached out and touched him, but she was too awe-struck to do anything but stare. Frannie never looked at her. He never uttered a word. He just went by, looking straight ahead with an earnest, almost determined look on his face. Helen followed his movements as if entranced.

When Frannie reached the back yard, he stooped down and appeared to dig around some rosebushes Bill had bought Helen the week before. He then stood up, walked over to the grape arbor in one corner of the yard, and was lost from view among the shadows.

Rushing over to her husband's bed, Helen exclaimed, "Bill, Frannie's alive! I just saw him go by the window. He's under the grape arbor right now!"

Bill sat up, rubbed his eyes, and told his wife she must be having a nightmare. But Helen refused to be put off. She was so insistent, in fact, that Bill agreed to investigate.

Putting on their bathrobes the couple hurried to the back yard and searched under the grape arbor. There was no one in sight! Bill was about to say, "I told you so," when Helen remembered seeing Frannie doing something around the rosebushes and suggested they take a look.

Now it was Bill's turn to be surprised. He knew the rosebushes hadn't "taken" and that Helen had planned to dig them up that very day but hadn't done so because of her son's death. But now, as he looked at the plants in the moonlight, he was dumbfounded. So was Helen. Not only were the plants alive; they were blooming!

This experience firmly convinced the Schmidts that Frannie

was alive and conscious—and that he wanted them to know it.

But these are not the only evidences for soul or spirit survival.

Channeling

Recently a new fad called "channeling" has caught on in various parts of the world. Popularized by actress Shirley MacLaine, it is the practice of communicating with the spirits of the dead through mediums or "channelers" as they are called. In her book *Out on a Limb,* Miss MacLaine tells how Kevin Ryerson had his first channeling experience and what convinced him that a "discarnate entity" had spoken through him.

Here is what she quotes him as saying:

[A] spirit came through during one of my meditations. I didn't even know it. But someone ran and got a tape recorder and got the whole thing. When they played it back to me I freaked. I knew nothing about the medical information I had channeled through. I didn't know the voices that came through me either, and I certainly didn't make up the past-life information while fabricating a phony voice.[2]

Conclusions

Instances such as these, and others that seem even more persuasive, have convinced many people that the dead are conscious and that under certain circumstances are able to communicate with the living.

This sense of identity provides the ability to experience one's self as something that has continuity and sameness.

—Erik Homburger Erikson in *Childhood and Society*

Chapter 2
Identity

Something Out There

Interest in psychic phenomena has been increasing in recent years. For example, on August 10, 1987, the Associated Press reported that "scientists who investigate such mysteries as psychic spoon-bending, mind-reading and things that go bump in the night wound up an international conference [in Edinburgh, Scotland on] Saturday [August 9], saying *there is something out there, but they aren't sure what.*" (Emphasis supplied.)[1] More recently parapsychologists from all over the world met in Florida with the express intention of making contact with the spirits of the dead.

Many skeptics, while admitting that strange things happen, insist that all paranormal phenomena can be explained on the basis of universally recognized natural laws.[2] On the other hand, believers in soul-survival maintain that at least some of these phenomena are produced by entities called souls or spirits. Opinions on the subject abound and the argument tends to run hot.

Most people who believe in soul- or spirit-survival do so on the basis of religious beliefs. They merely *assume* that consciousness survives death without any concrete evidence to support this assumption. However, New Agers (an umbrella term for various avant garde groups, some of whom profess to make contact with spirit entities), Spiritualists, and some parapsychologists (privately, of course) offer what they claim is credible evidence for the survival of personal consciousness after bodily death.

Definitions and Explanations

Unlike materialists who maintain that consciousness is the function of the brain, soul-survivalists hold that consciousness is the *function of an invisible entity* called the soul or spirit. This entity is believed to inhabit the body in life and separate from it at death. THIS IS THE CRUX OF THE SOUL-SURVIVAL AND REINCARNATION THEORIES.

Generally speaking the terms *soul* and *spirit* are quasi-synonymous and are often used interchangeably. But there is a difference. *Spirit* usually refers to any invisible intelligence, whereas *souls* are limited to human spirits.

Soul-survivalists claim that under conditions little understood spirit entities can make themselves visible. Such phenomena are called materializations. When the soul or spirit leaves a living body and later returns to it, the phenomenon is called an out-of-body experience (OBE) or astral projection.

According to soul-survivalist theory, in the case of an OBE the soul has begun separating from the body, but returns to it since resuscitation efforts have been successful. However, when the dying process reaches the point of no return this separation becomes complete; and the soul or spirit, which is conceived to be immortal, lives on as an independent entity.

A large number, perhaps a majority, of soul-survivalists believe that after a time the soul enters another body, where it continues its existence. This is called metempsychosis or, more commonly, reincarnation. Continued existence implies, of course, continued identity, for soul-survivalists insist that the identity of the soul or spirit transcends death, and unless this is true, talk about soul-survival is meaningless.

Soul-Survivalist Claims

Long ago, soul-survivalist Emma Hardinge Britten asserted the indestructibility of the soul or spirit in these terms:

We have found beyond a shadow of doubt or peradventure, that death had no power over the Spirit, could never touch the soul, or destroy one attribute or property of soul life.[3]

This is a momentous assertion. If true, it is the most precious truth ever revealed a grieving humanity; if false, it is the most shameless fraud ever perpetrated in the name of life's tenderest memories!

The Identity Problem

Laying aside the naturalistic explanations of skeptics, and accepting the soul-survivalist premise that invisible intelligences do exist, the question is: How can one be certain "beyond a shadow of doubt or peradventure" that entities, whose normal state of existence lies outside our world of sensory experience, are, in fact, the entities they purport to be? To ask the question is to answer it. No one can be sure.

This conclusion is confirmed by Archie Matson, a soul-survivalist who attended a séance put on by medium Arthur Ford, when he says he conversed with four spirits who claimed they were former acquaintances, yet admits that he had "no way of being sure they were actually the persons the voice coming through the sleeping Ford claimed them to be."[4]

If these spirits were not Matson's former acquaintances, is it possible that they were impersonating spirits trying to deceive him?

Remarkable Admission

Sir Arthur Conan Doyle of Sherlock Holmes fame, speaking of the spirits of the dead with whom he professed to communicate, once confessed: "We have unhappily, to deal with absolute coldblooded lying on the part of wicked or mischievous intelligences."[5]

More recently Brenda Crenshaw, a Los Angeles psychic, conceded that "there are spirits who are impersonators . . . [who] will come through a medium to make claims that are not true."[6]

The authoritative *Encyclopedia of Occultism & Parapsychol-*

ogy acknowledges that "there are plenty of communications attributed to deceiving spirits."[7]

What an admission! Some spirits lie and impersonate!

Impostors?

When human beings are dealing with human impostors, it is often difficult (sometimes impossible) to detect their fraud—*even when physical evidence is available*. But, when human beings are dealing with intelligences that exist outside our world of perception, at least some of whom lie and impersonate, *the problem of identity becomes critical*. Need it be said that, if these entities lie, they possess enormous powers to deceive?

Reasoning from these facts, it is evident that, since at least some of the spirits are deceivers, the so-called "proofs" of soul-survivalists are not "beyond a shadow of doubt or peradventure."

What If . . . ?

But if spirit intelligences were to submit to rigorously controlled scientific tests, wouldn't this establish their identity beyond a reasonable doubt? Unfortunately, it would not, and the reason for this is that, even if such entities *appeared* to submit to scientific tests, they might be manipulating the evidence behind the scenes (undetected by human beings, of course)—*the better to deceive*!

This conclusion seems to put the identification of spirit entities outside the realm of possibility. And yet, as will be shown, there is a way to positively determine who these beings are. This will be dealt with in a later chapter, but first let us examine the matter of human consciousness and near-death experiences (NDEs).

Because consciousness is so difficult to define, psychologists have concentrated on exploring states of consciousness (trance, meditation, sleep) markedly different from our normal waking state.
—*The ABC of Psychology*, Leonard Kristal, general editor

Chapter 3

The Mystery of Consciousness

An Analogy

Have you ever tried to lift yourself by your bootstraps? If you haven't, try it. It can't be done. In a similar way trying to define consciousness without using the word *consciousness* or one of its synonyms, is to attempt the impossible. And yet, while we may not be able to define consciousness, we know perfectly well what we mean by the term—*by experience.*

The reason for this paradox seems to be as follows: If consciousness (that which knows) is of a higher order than that which is known (the physical world around us, for instance), *that which knows can never know itself*—at least not fully.

But going back to the bootstraps. Although we may never fully understand consciousness, the analogy suggests that just as we can lift one boot at a time, so we can understand something about consciousness, without ever being able to understand it fully.

Perhaps an example or two at this point will help illustrate the subtle and mysterious nature of consciousness.

India's Rip Van Winkle

Up until July 1944 Mr. Bhopalchand Lodha of Jodpur, India, worked as a public-works secretary for his native state. He enjoyed good health and had the reputation of being an excellent worker. However, through some bureaucratic mixup, he was suspended from his position for "misconduct in service."

15

Lodha was understandably upset. He immediately telephoned the chief minister of public works, who set a hearing date six weeks from the day Lodha called.

During the phone conversation Lodha became dizzy and subsequently complained of not feeling well. While awaiting the inquiry, he became extremely tense and had two sharp bouts with malarial fever. Not long before the hearing he sank into a deep sleep. Yet his heart continued to beat normally and his respiratory and alimentary systems continued to function as usual. And yet, so far as any conscious responses were concerned, Lodha could have passed for dead.

Lodha's sensations and deep reflexes disappeared completely, and doctors agree that, but for the faithful ministrations of his wife and children, one of whom was a physician, Mr. Lodha would not have lived long. *He remained unconscious for over seven and a half years!*

Suddenly, on the evening of January 4, 1952, Lodha had another malarial attack. His temperature shot up, then subsided. It shot up again, and went down once more. Soon after this, his fingers moved slightly, then his toes. After more time passed, his eyelids fluttered. A month later he could turn his head and swallow. After several more months, he was able to see, but could not recognize his children because of the changes that had taken place in them in the intervening years. It took a whole year for him to regain full consciousness, but regain it he did!

Of his more than seven-and-a-half-year sleep, Lodha could remember *absolutely nothing.* He was completely unaware, for instance, that during his long sleep his father had died in the same house.[1]

Where was Lodha's soul or spirit all this time?

Transient Global Amnesia

Several years ago I had an episode of what doctors call transient global amnesia or TGA. I remember waking up one morning feeling fine. I had an appointment to meet a friend at the local airport where we were to take a plane to Mountain View, California. Before I left for my appointment my wife and I picked some raspberries in our back yard. That is the last thing I clearly remember doing that morning, except for one incident which will be mentioned later.

Whenever possible, I try to meet my appointments a few minutes before the agreed time. That particular morning Vesta tells me I acted as if I had all the time in the world. I had begun to have a TGA. The conversation and the description of the events that follow are reconstructed from what Vesta remembers of the episode.

When Vesta noticed that I wasn't getting ready for my trip, she said, "Don, don't you think you should be dressing to go to the airport?"

"What for?" I asked.

"Have you forgotten your appointment?"

"What appointment?"

"Your appointment to fly with Will Richards to Mountain View."

"This is the first I've heard about it."

For a few moments Vesta thought I was "pulling her leg." But before long she realized that something was wrong with my ability to remember. At her urging I finally got dressed, and she drove us to the airport. On the way I asked, "Where are we going?" and she answered, "We're going to the airport to meet Will Richards." But no sooner had she finished her explanation than I asked again, "Where are we going?" She says this happened at least a half dozen times. Toward the end she says I even said, "Now I have it straight"—only to repeat my previous question moments later.

At the airport Vesta says I seemed a bit embarrassed when I met Will and she explained to him that something was wrong with my ability to remember. She thought I might have had a slight stroke and said she didn't think I should go on the trip.

After telling Will goodbye, Vesta took me to the local hospital, where Dr. Roger Curran administered some tests and had me undergo a CAT scan. Somehow, I don't know how or why, I remember being inside that machine, or at least I think I do. I say this because this figment may be something I later reconstructed from what Vesta told me. I do not know. Everything else is a total blank.

Several hours later, when I regained my memory, Vesta told me what had happened. One of the first things I did was to try to remember what Dr. Curran looked like. But try as I might I could not dredge up a single mental image of the man.

A week later I went to Dr. Curran's office for a checkup. Although I could not remember what he looked like, I wondered if seeing him would stimulate any latent memories. When I arrived at his office and read his "shingle," I suddenly realized that my experiment was not going to be as simple as I had anticipated. Dr. Curran worked with two associates.

While pondering this complication, a man, obviously a medical doctor, walked past the door behind the receptionist. If this was Dr. Curran, I couldn't recall having ever seen him. A few minutes later another physician walked past the same spot. I only saw his profile, but I knew instantly it was Dr. Curran. How did I know? I haven't the foggiest idea. It could have been Dr. Curran's other associate, but I knew without the shadow of a doubt that it was Dr. Curran and not someone else.

While Dr. Curran was checking me over, I told him about my recognizing him although I had no visual remembrance of having ever seen him before. He had no explanation. Consciousness is a strange thing.

Oh, incidentally, Dr. Curran assured me that although medical science at present did not know what caused TGAs, they seldom recur, but if they do recur, they usually happen within a few days following the episode. I was glad to hear that, but the mysterious nature of consciousness still baffles me—and I am not the only one mystified by it.

A Higher Authority Needed

Other even more striking examples of the mysterious nature of consciousness could doubtless be given, but perhaps the foregoing episodes will be considered sufficient to illustrate how little we know about this strange phenomenon. We may know many things about how it functions, but like the uncertainty principle of physics, we are so inextricably involved with consciousness when we try to analyze it that we cannot determine its fundamental nature.

From this it seems reasonable to conclude that, if we are ever to understand what it is that gives rise to consciousness, it must be revealed to us by a consciousness superior to our own. But before appealing to such an authority, let us examine the matter of OBEs, believed by many to be one of the most persuasive evidences of soul-survival.

At that moment, she saw herself floating out of her physical body, floating a few feet above her body. She was very surprised at seeing her corpse in that bed.

—Elizabeth Kübler-Ross in *Death Does Not Exist*

Chapter 4

Out-of-Body Experiences

Not All the Dying Have OBEs

Several years ago Stuart Nelson, a physician friend of mine, fell while working on his house. No one seems to know exactly what happened, but apparently he lost his footing and dropped some eight feet and landed on his head. His wife, a registered nurse, carefully dragged him to the family car, laid him on the back seat, and rushed him to the hospital. There his colleagues put forth heroic efforts to save his life. Twice they thought he had slipped beyond their grasp, but each time they succeeded in bringing him back from the brink of death.

Some time later, when I talked to Dr. Nelson, I asked him if he had experienced anything that could be described as a near-death vision or an OBE. He said he had not. He stated unequivocally that everything was a total blank between the time he fell and the time he recovered consciousness nineteen days later. He said that the first thing he remembered on coming to was finding himself home suffering from a bad headache.

Dr. Nelson's experience is not singular. Researchers in the NDE field candidly admit that "not everyone who has a brush with death has a classical near-death vision or even a partial OBE, with only some of the major components. [Psychologist Kenneth] Ring has found that approximately 51 percent of illness and accident victims had an NDE, a figure not too divergent from that reported by [Michael B.] Sabom [M.D.] and [Sarah] Kreutziger [M.S.W.]."[1]

So, only about half of those who have a brush with death

have a near-death experience of any kind. This is strange. One would think that, if NDEs corresponded to reality and, therefore, were evidence of soul-survival, NDEs would be experienced by everyone who came near death and escaped. But this is not the case. Why?

The Seat of Consciousness

As indicated earlier, believers in soul-survival hold that mind or consciousness is not a function of the brain, but rather, the function of a nonphysical entity which they call the soul or spirit. This entity is believed to inhabit the body in life and function *through* the brain. Here is how some soul-survivalists express this point of view:

> That there is a close relationship between the body and mind [i.e., consciousness] a very little experience shows. If a piece of shell hits my skull and damages the grey matter within it, I may lose the power of speech or of the movement of my limbs. On the other hand, if I take a child who is dull to a physician and let him be treated with certain glandular extracts, I shall find that the deficiency in intelligence passes away and the child becomes possessed of normal mentality. But whilst this is true, it does not mean that mind can be interpreted as a function of brain. What it does mean is that brain is the instrument of mind, and that the more efficient the instrument the more completely will mind be able to communicate its ideas and perceptions.[2]

Another soul-survivalist expresses the same belief in these words:

> The real person or soul centres in the spirit body, and only temporarily uses and expresses itself through the physical body which is its creation and shadow.[3]

This theory sounds plausible, but something may sound plausible without being true.

The fact that a blow to the head can temporarily obliterate

consciousness suggests that consciousness is intimately associated with the brain. Soul-survivalist, David H. Lund, says:

> Science has gone further in showing that damage to specific areas of the brain result in the elimination or impairment of particular mental capacities and that the capacities for seeing, hearing, tasting, smelling and touching are connected, in the case of each, with a different region of the brain. Drugs such as LSD, mescaline, psilocybin, and heroin alter consciousness in a profound way by altering brain and body chemistry. And when portions of the brain are radically disconnected with [sic, from] the rest, as in the case of a prefrontal lobotomy, significant changes in consciousness and personality result.[4]

If consciousness were the function of a nonphysical entity, as soul-survivalists claim, why should brain impairment have any effect on it whatever? After all, soul-survivalists claim that after death consciousness continues to function *without the brain*!

Ingenious arguments advanced to explain how consciousness, which cannot function normally through a partially impaired brain, can function quite adequately after the brain is totally impaired by death, do not seem especially convincing.

Psychedelic Drugs and Out-of-Body Experiences

As already suggested, several things besides brain injury can affect consciousness. Many drugs can alter it—and some of these drugs can produce OBEs *in some people*. Furthermore, these experiences are not limited to persons on the threshold of death.

For example: Dr. Timothy Leary of psychedelic-drug fame, after eating certain Mexican mushrooms, is quoted as reporting: "I realized that I had died, that I, Timothy Leary, the Timothy Leary game [sic], was gone. I could look back and see my body in bed."[5]

Dr. Leary, of course, had not died. He only imagined he had. He was hallucinating.

Author Aldous Huxley, after taking mescaline, wrote: "My

body seemed to have dissociated itself almost completely from my mind. . . . It was odd, of course, to feel that 'I' was not the same as these arms and legs 'out there.' "[6]

One individual who took LSD reported: "My ideas of space were strange beyond description. I could see myself from head to foot as well as the sofa on which I was lying."[7]

As previously pointed out, not everyone who ingests or injects psychedelic substances into his body has an OBE. Some do and some don't, and no one seems to know exactly why.

Carbon Dioxide and OBEs

Other chemicals besides psychedelic drugs can cause OBEs. High concentrations of carbon dioxide in the blood, called hypercapnia, can in some instances produce the same effect.

In one experiment Dr. Ladislas J. Meduna administered 30 percent carbon dioxide and 70 percent oxygen to a subject. After the experiment, he quotes the subject as saying: "I felt as though I was looking down at myself, as though I was way out here in space. . . . I felt sort of separated."[8]

Another subject to whom he administered CO_2 reported: "I felt myself being separated; my soul, drawing apart from the physical being, was drawn upward seemingly to leave the earth and to go upward where it reached a greater Spirit with whom there was a communion, producing a remarkable, new relaxation and deep security."[9]

Carbon dioxide is a natural product of the body's metabolic processes. Normally it is exhaled when we breathe. But when respiration stops or is greatly reduced, it remains in the tissues and bloodstream and may well be an important factor in causing near-death visions.

The Fissure of Sylvius

But there are other things besides NDEs, psychedelic drugs, and hypercapnia that can produce OBEs. Neurosurgeons have discovered that stimulating certain areas of the cerebral cortex with tiny electric probes can produce OBEs. Thus, Dr. Melvin Morse and his colleagues report:

There is clear evidence that within the temporal lobe

there are neuronal connections that, when electrically stimulated, produce the sensation of being outside the physical body. For example, a 33-year-old man suffered from temporal lobe seizures that produced hallucinations of seeing himself. On electrical stimulation within the fissure of Sylvius, the patient exclaimed, "Oh, God, I am leaving my body."[10]

This is intriguing. But notice, such stimulation produces the "sensation," not the reality, of being outside the physical body. In other words, patients who have these experiences are hallucinating.

Furthermore, what is true of NDEs, psychedelic drugs, and high concentrations of CO_2, is true of electrical stimulation of the cerebral cortex—not everyone has an OBE.

Belief in Soul-Survival and OBEs

Could it be that a person's beliefs have at least some bearing on who is likely to have an OBE? Could it be that a person who believes in soul-survival is *more likely* to have an OBE than one who does not? The answer seems to be Yes.

Researchers Drs. Ian Stevenson and Bruce Greyson report:

> A comparison of accounts of near-death experiences obtained in different cultures suggests that the beliefs a person has *before* he approaches death have an important influence on the kind of experience he will report if he comes close to death and escapes.[11] (Emphasis supplied.)

This is significant. It means that if a Buddhist has a near-death vision, it will *tend* to be in harmony with Buddhist beliefs; if a Moslem has a near-death vision, it will *tend* to accord with Islamic beliefs; if someone from a Christian culture has a near-death vision, it will *tend* to correspond to his particular Christian beliefs.

This conclusion is confirmed by another study done by Drs. Satwant Pasricha and Ian Stevenson, in which a comparison is made between OBEs in India and America. These researchers state unequivocally that "the difference in the NDE experiences *correspond with different prevailing ideas about life after death* in India and the United States."[12] (Emphasis supplied.)

This is illuminating! Psychedelic drugs, high concentrations of CO_2, and electrical stimulation of the temporal lobe are physical factors that can be scientifically controlled and measured. But what a person believes is a subjective experience—and this is difficult if not impossible to control externally. And yet, what a person believes, perhaps even subconsciously, apparently has an influence on whether or not it is possible for him to have an OBE.

Anxiety and Depersonalization

Another quasi-subjective factor involved in near-death visions is anxiety. In the summary of an article published by Dr. Russell Noyes and colleagues, this statement is made:

> Anxiety was significantly associated with the development of depersonalization [defined as "altered-awareness-of-self visions"] among psychiatric patients and was almost certainly a factor among accident victims. The findings suggest that this syndrome is *a specific response to extreme danger or its associated anxiety.*[13] (Emphasis supplied.)

So another factor in these altered-awareness-of-self visions are extreme danger or its associated anxiety.

Natural and Supernatural OBEs

Although the vast majority of OBEs discussed above can perhaps be explained on the basis of physical laws and natural subjective factors, they may not explain all OBEs. For instance, in an interview famous psychiatrist and author/lecturer Gerald Jampolsky reported having an OBE in which apparently none of the physical factors were involved. It happened during a meeting with Swami Muktananda. Said Jampolsky:

> He touched me with peacock feathers. I began to have the impression that our minds were joined. He touched

me again on the head with his hand.

After this, beautiful colors appeared all around me, and it seemed as though I had stepped out of my body and was looking down at it.[14]

Astral Projection

Other experiences are perhaps even more impressive. The *Handbook of Parapsychology*, states that "in a very few number of cases, the phantasm of the experient [the one having the OBE] has been observed at the locality which he seemed to himself to have visited during his OBE."[15]

Is it possible that in some cases of OBE spirit entities stimulate the cerebral cortex of the experient and thus induce the hallucination? If human beings can do this electrically, what is to prevent spirit entities from doing the same in ways unknown to us?

Is it possible that in those instances of OBE, in which the experient is physically observed to be located in one place, yet perceives himself to be in another—*and is apparently seen by others to be in the second location*—that both the experient and the observers are the subject of an elaborate deception produced by seducing spirits?

Conclusion

Who can say? But at least everyone can agree with researcher Sabom, who, though he seems to advocate soul-survival, concedes that OBE "experiences are not by themselves prima facie evidence of life after death."[16] Thus the nature of consciousness remains a mystery.

Most wondrous book! bright candle of the Lord!
Star of eternity! The only star
By which the bark of man could navigate
The sea of life, and gain the coast of bliss securely.
                              —Pollock in *Course of Time*

Chapter 5

The Touchstone

In June 1933 a man dying of a heart condition in a Chicago hospital asked his doctors to notify his son, who lived on the West Coast, that he was not expected to live long and urge him to come to his bedside as soon as possible. His reason? He had an important secret he wanted to pass on to him.

In those days many of the life-support systems we take for granted today were unknown, but Drs. Albert S. Hyman and E. Fritz of the Watkins Foundation had developed a technique that was capable of restarting a stopped heart. It consisted of a long hollow needle which Dr. Hyman inserted into the dying man's heart muscle, through which he injected stimulants, essential nutrients, and transmitted a weak, pulsating electric current to the vital organ.

While the patient waited for his son to arrive, his heart stopped. Back in 1933 a person in this condition was reckoned to be "biologically, medically, physically and legally dead." Accordingly, this man "died" and came back to life, not once, but several times because Dr. Hyman was able to restart his heart again and again. As a result the man lived long enough to pass on his important secret.

Our curiosity is piqued. What could the momentous secret have been? So far as I am aware no one knows. But according to the newspaper report many people, especially clergymen, wondered what the man had to say about life after death.[1] This curiosity about death is not surprising. From time immemorial religious people have believed that death was not the end of conscious existence. But proof for this belief has remained illusive.

The Hallmark of Religion

Many people suppose that belief in a God or gods is the distinguishing mark of religion. This is incorrect. Many of the most primitive religious cults have no concept of lesser gods, let alone of a Supreme Being—*yet their devotees profess to hold communion with the spirits of the dead!*

On the other hand, virtually every religion teaches or at least gives lip service to belief in life after death—*whether this is because the soul is immortal, or because there is to be a resurrection from the dead.* It is this belief that distinguishes religion from that larger body of knowledge known as philosophy. Some philosophies, as everyone knows, deny any kind of life after death.

It should come as no surprise, therefore, that a careful examination of the world's religions reveals that this persistent belief runs the gamut from the most uncivilized cult to the most sophisticated creed. *It is, in fact, the hallmark of religion.*

Immortality or Resurrection?

Most Christians believe in the resurrection of the body—or at least they give lip service to it. This is why the followers of Christ have Easter Sunday sunrise services. Another way Christians show their belief in the resurrection is by their recitation of the Apostles' Creed. This creed says, among other things:

> I believe . . . in Jesus Christ . . . who . . . shall come to judge the quick and the dead. [*I believe in*] . . . the resurrection of the body . . . [and the life everlasting].[2]

But the strange thing is that many of these same Christians insist that man's soul goes to its reward at death. However, if the soul is the "real" person, why encumber it with a resurrected body? Furthermore, if the soul goes to its reward at death, what need is there for a resurrection, a second coming, a future judgment?

The Touchstone of Truth

In former times dealers in precious metals tested gold and silver by examining the streak these metals left when they were rubbed across a black siliceous rock called touchstone. In a similar way, the Christian who wishes to know the truth about life after death will consult the Bible to see whether or not his beliefs agree with what it teaches. Christians believe that this Book was written under the inspiration of the Creator of consciousness, and, therefore, what it reveals concerning the nature of conscious existence is true.

In the next chapter we shall see what the Bible has to say about the soul and spirit.

What is man, that thou art mindful of him?

—Psalm 8:4

Chapter 6

Human Nature

Several years ago the conservative, evangelical magazine *Christianity Today* carried an article by David G. Myers entitled "ESP and the Paranormal: Supernatural or Superfraud?" In it Myers says:

> Although many Christian writers have touted ESP [extrasensory perception] as proof of a nonmaterial essence in human nature, books and articles along these lines usually display a seeming ignorance—ignorance about the scientific status of ESP, and ignorance about the emerging biblical conceptions of human nature as a bounded mind-body unity. Investigations of the correspondence between our brain states and our emotions, thoughts, and actions indicate that the mind is linked to the body as closely as is a telephone message to the electrical events in the phone line. This modern view parallels the ancient holistic view of the Hebrew people, expressed also in the radical Christian hope of a resurrected mind-body unit.[1]

This is an important statement. Does the Bible, in fact, teach what the author of the above article says it teaches? Let us see.

Basis of Study

The average person reading this book probably cannot read the Scriptures in the original languages. If he wishes to study a biblical subject in depth, he will probably have to use one of many translations of the Bible that have been made from the Hebrew-Aramaic and Greek originals. To simplify this task, the King James Version (hereinafter abbreviated KJV) will be used as a basis for comparing and analyzing the various words rendered *soul* and *spirit,* in their singular as well as their plural forms.

The reason the KJV has been selected is simply that it is generally recognized as a good translation, and further, it constitutes the basis of by far the largest number of readily available Bible commentaries, concordances, lexicons, and Bible dictionaries in the English language—a fact that will facilitate additional study by anyone who wishes to pursue the subject further.

Statistical Facts and Observations

The English words *soul* and *spirit* occur a total of 1,056 times in the KJV. These words are translated from five Hebrew-Aramaic and three Greek words. The Hebrew-Aramaic words are *nephesh, ruach, neshamah, nedibah,* and *ob*; the Greek words are *psuche, pneuma,* and *phantasma.*

These original words occur 1,677 times in the text from which the KJV was translated. Of these eight words, *nedibah* occurs only once. It is a mistranslation, and since it does not relate to man's constituent nature or to life after death, it will not be considered in this study. *Phantasma* occurs only twice and is the word from which we get our word *phantom.* Although in both instances it is translated "spirit," it does not relate to man's constituent nature and hence will not be considered for the same reason. *Ob* occurs sixteen times and is always rendered "familiar spirit(s)." Since it too does not relate to man's constituent nature, it will not be considered at this point, but it will be touched on later. This leaves 1,658 instances in which the original words frequently deal with man's constituent nature.

The five original words that remain occur with the following frequency: *nephesh,* 754 times; *ruach,* 389; *neshamah,* 25; *psuche,* 105; and *pneuma,* 385, for the total of 1,658.

Of this number the KJV translates *nephesh* "soul" 472 times;

psuche "soul" 58; *ruach* "spirit" 237; *pneuma* "spirit" 286; and *neshamah* "soul" once and "spirit" twice, for the total of 1,056 times.

In the remaining 602 occurrences these original words are translated by 71 other English words or phrases.[2]

Significance

The significance of these facts is that whenever possible the translators of the KJV rendered the five original words under consideration by the English words *soul* and *spirit*.

But now notice: Of the 1,658 occurrences of the original words, *not once* did the KJV scholars translate *nephesh* or *psuche,* "spirit," *nor did they ever* render *ruach* or *pneuma,* "soul." In other words, these scholars made a clear distinction between these two sets of words. From this fact one concludes that the KJV scholars considered *soul* to be the closest equivalent of *nephesh* and *psuche,* and that *spirit* was the closest equivalent of *ruach* and *pneuma.*

The KJV scholars are not alone making this distinction. Other translators and scholars have in large measure followed their lead. This distinction reflects a fundamental difference between the two sets of original words—*even though in some instances they superficially appear to be synonymous.*

Some Words Convey Underlying Concepts

Everyone familiar with English knows that a word may convey more than one meaning. Many examples of such words could be given, but perhaps one will be considered sufficient to illustrate the point.

Take the word *time.* It can mean "measured or measurable duration." It can mean "a period when something occurred"—the time when such and such happened. It can refer to "the reckoning of duration"—to time something. It can mean "tempo," as in music—the rhythm and speed of a piece of music. And so on. Now, what is true of English words is equally true of the Hebrew-Aramaic and Greek words under consideration. They, too, can have a variety of meanings.

However, even though a word has many shades of meaning, it frequently happens that it continues to carry with it a common denominator. This is true of the word *time* in the above example. Thus, although *time* has a variety of meanings, all of them relate in one way or another to that nonphysical continuum we call time. In a similar way, although the Hebrew-Aramaic and Greek words being considered are translated by a wide variety of meanings, these many meanings continue to convey certain underlying concepts, or what we might call common denominators.

Common Denominator Underlying *Nephesh* and *Psuche*

A comparison of the various uses of *nephesh* in the Old Testament and *psuche* in the New Testament shows that the common denominator underlying the biblical uses of these terms is that of "individuality." They will therefore be referred to in this study as *nephesh/psuche*, although at times they will be treated separately.

Most often these words refer to the individual as a discrete unit of conscious existence. However, sometimes part of the individual is used to represent the whole person, or the whole individual is used to represent only a part of him. When a word is used in this way it is called a synechdoche.

We use synechdoches all the time but seldom think about it. Take the expression "There were 200 hands on the ship." When we say "hand" in this context we don't literally mean 200 hands. We mean that the ship's crew consisted of 200 men.

In a similar way, while *nephesh/psuche* usually stand for the individual, at times the individual's life-principle stands for the whole person. When this is the case, it is usually translated "life." In other instances *nephesh/psuche* are translated "mind," meaning the individual's consciousness.

(For all biblical occurrences of *nephesh/psuche*, see Appendix A.)

Common Denominator Underlying *Ruach* and *Pneuma*

A comparison of the uses of *ruach* and *pneuma* reveals that the concept underlying this set of biblical terms is that of an "invisible agent." An agent is either an impersonal force or a personal entity that acts—usually in a manner perceptible to the senses. It is not surprising, therefore, to find the Bible using *ruach* and *pneuma* to mean wind or angels, for instance, since both of these are invisible agents.

In a similar way these words can signify the life-principle. This form of divine energy is also an invisible agent—one that manifests itself in and through living things. But, now notice. When *ruach/pneuma* convey the idea of life, they refer to that form of divine power or force that is present in *all* living things, not simply the individual, whereas, when *nephesh/psuche* are used to mean life they refer to *individualized* life.

Ruach/pneuma frequently apply to members of the Godhead, especially the Holy Spirit, who usually operates behind the scenes as an invisible agent. As previously mentioned, these words may also refer to angelic beings, either good or bad, because they, too, are invisible agents. Sometimes these words even signify the mind as the invisible motivator of human activity.

It is significant that while *ruach/pneuma* frequently mean mind as the invisible motivator of human activity, nowhere is consciousness attributed to these words *after death*.

(For all biblical occurrences of *ruach/pneuma* see Appendix B.)

Common Denominator Underlying *Neshamah*

The last of the five original words under consideration, *neshamah*, is rendered once "soul" and "spirit" twice. Most of the time it is translated "breath." When it means breath as the sign of the presence of the life-principle in living persons, it is virtually synonymous with *ruach*. The Old Testament frequently uses it this way.

As with *nephesh/psuche* and *ruach/pneuma*, in not a single instance does the Bible call *neshamah* immortal or say it is conscious after death.

(For all biblical occurrences of *neshamah* see Appendix C.)

Man's Constituent Nature

The Bible associates *nephesh/psuche*, *ruach/pneuma*, and *neshamah* with the constituent nature of human beings.

This is how the Hebrew-Aramaic words are used to describe Adam's creation:

"The Lord God formed man of the dust of the ground, and breathed into his nostrils the breath of life [*neshamah chaiyyim*, literally ' breath of lives']; and man became a living soul [*nephesh chayyah*, literally 'a soul of life']." Genesis 2:7.

It goes without saying that "breath of life" is not simply the air we breathe. No amount of air pumped into a lifeless corpse can restore it to life and consciousness. But breath or breathing is an evidence that the life-principle is present. Hence the Bible uses breath to symbolize the life-principle.

The Genesis 2:7 description of Adam's creation makes it clear that the first living, human soul was the product of two factors: "formed dust" and "breath of lives." Two ingredients: one, matter previously created by God and subsequently organized by Him into Adam's body; the other, breath of lives, the life-principle—that invisible agent which emanates from the Creator and is present in all living things were combined to constitute man a composite unit—"a living soul, a living individual."

The living soul, with the potential for conscious existence, was not the lifeless dust that was formed into Adam's body, nor was it the "breath of lives" common to all living creatures. It was that third "something"—*nephesh*—which Adam "became."

When the two components that went into making Adam came together, conscious existence became possible. The living soul was not "something" that existed before it "became." The Bible knows nothing of the preexistence of the soul.

Scholars Agree

Many biblical scholars agree with the above conclusion. Representative of them is Professor J. I. Marais, who, writing in the conservative *International Standard Bible Encyclopedia*, says:

> The Scripture states very clearly that life was inbreathed into man by God. . . . The human being thus inspired by God was hereby constituted a *nephesh [c]hayyah*

("living soul"), because *nishmath [c]hayyim* ("breath of lives") had been imparted to him (Gen. 2:7).[3]

The Light Bulb Analogy

The relationship that exists among the body, the breath of life, and the living soul is analogous to an electric light bulb, in which the body represents the bulb with its filament, the electric current the breath of life or life-principle, and the living soul the product of the two. When electricity flows through the tungsten filament, light, representing consciousness, is produced.

Parents Are Transmission Vehicles

That which the Bible teaches concerning Adam's constituent nature is true of his descendants, although the process is obviously different. This is why Job complains that God continues to vex his "soul [*nephesh*]; all the while my breath [*neshamah*] is in me, and the spirit [*ruach*] of God is in my nostrils." Job 27:2, 3.

Today we might paraphrase what Job says this way: "God continues to vex me (my *nephesh*) as long as I have breath (*neshamah*) and the life-principle (*ruach*) is in me."

The biblical teaching concerning man's nature clearly implies that parents are the vehicles through whom God transmits the components of life—body and breath of life—in order to constitute children "living souls." God is still the creator of the living soul, but He works indirectly through parents, whom He holds accountable for the children they bring into the world.

The Nature of Animals

That which the Bible reveals concerning the constituent nature of man is true of animals. The ingredients in both cases are the same. However, the process by which God created the animals differed from the way He created Adam. He did not give animals the "personal touch" He gave the father of the human race.

Notice how the Bible describes the creation of animals: "God said, Let the earth bring forth the living creature [*nephesh chayyah*, soul of life] after his kind, cattle, and creeping thing, and beast of the earth." Genesis 1:24.

Here the identical expression *nephesh chayyah* applied to Adam in Genesis 2:7 is applied to the animal creation.

The Contrast Between Soul and Spirit

Speaking of the similarity between the constituent nature of men and animals, A. E. Garvie states in his *Dictionary of the Bible*:

> A contrast between soul and spirit may be recognized; while the latter is the *universal principle* imparting life from the Creator, the former is the *individual organism* possessed of life in the creature.[4] (Emphasis supplied.)

Formula for Conscious Existence

Clearly the biblical formula for living soul with the potential for conscious existence, whether human or an animal, is simply: Body + life-principle from God = living soul.

Man Is More Than an Animal

Does this mean that man is nothing more than an animal? No it does not. It does mean, however, that men and animals are made of the same components. However, man was given a "divine touch" when he was created; the animals were not. Man was created in the image of God with a moral consciousness; the animals were not.

In the next chapter we shall see what the Bible has to say about the soul and immortality.

What profit [is there] in my death if I go down into the pit? Can the dust confess thee or proclaim thy truth?

—Psalm 30:9, NEB

Chapter 7

Search for the Immortal Soul

Ethan Allen and the Ghost

It is said that Ethan Allen, the Revolutionary War hero, courted the widow Buchanan as a young man. In order to reach home more quickly after his evening trysts, he fell into the habit of taking a shortcut through the local cemetery. Some of his pious New England neighbors noticed his practice and felt he was being a bit irreverent. So they conspired to teach the young man a lesson.

One of the plotters had noticed that Allen always vaulted the cemetery's cobblestone wall at exactly the same place every evening and suggested that they dig a grave at that spot. The next day, unbeknown to Allen, of course, they carried out their plan.

That evening, when our hero nimbly cleared the cemetery wall, he landed in a heap at the bottom of the excavation. Unharmed (dignity excepted), Allen quickly regained his footing and was preparing to surface, when a ghostly figure draped in a white sheet peered down at him and asked in a sepulchral tone of voice, "Ethan Allen, what art thou doing in my grave?"

With a trace of irritation Allen retorted, "Sir, that is not the question! The question is: What in thunder art thou doing out of it?"

Perhaps you smile at Allen's apt riposte. I did the first time I heard it. But the important thing is that it brings into focus a serious question: What, according to the Bible, happens to the soul and spirit when a person dies?

Souls Can Die or Be Destroyed

Some Christians are surprised to discover that the Bible sometimes calls a person's dead body, a soul, a *nephesh*. Here are a couple of examples: Haggai 2:13 says, "If one that is unclean by a dead body [*nephesh*] touch any of these [things], shall it be unclean?" Numbers 6:6 says that a Nazirite "shall come at no dead body [*nephesh*]." This use of *nephesh* occurs several more times in the Old Testament.

This biblical usage is not surprising since the Bible plainly teaches that the soul, rather than being immortal, is mortal, i.e., is subject to death. Thus, Ezekiel 18:20 plainly says, "The soul [*nephesh*] that sinneth, it shall die."

The New Testament is just as explicit in its teaching concerning *psuche*. Here are some examples: "Every living soul died in the sea." Revelation 16:3. "He which converteth the sinner from the error of his way, shall save a soul from death." James 5:20. "Every soul, which will not hear that prophet, shall be destroyed from among the people." Acts 3:23. Not only can the soul die, it can be destroyed. Instead of being immortal, it is subject to death.

Only God Is Inherently Immortal

Not only does the Bible teach that the soul is mortal, but it explicitly declares that God "only hath immortality [*athanasia*, deathlessness, immortality]." 1 Timothy 6:16. This means that if a human being ever attains to immortality, it is not because he has an immortal soul, but because by the grace of God "this mortal shall have *put on* immortality." 1 Corinthians 15:54. (Emphasis supplied.) This is a transformation that takes place, not at death, but at the second coming of Christ. (Cf. 1 Corinthians 15:22, 23, 51-54 with 1 Thessalonians 4:16, 17.)

The Scriptures teach that "immortality" [*aphtharsia*, incorruption] is not man's natural or inherent possession; it is something he is to "seek for." Romans 2:7. "Immortality" is a truth "brought . . . to light [not through the speculations of philosophy, but by revelation] through the gospel" of Jesus Christ. 2 Timothy 1:10.

It is true that everlasting or eternal life is the present possession of every believer in Christ, but eternal life is not a conscious entity; it is "the gift of God . . . through Jesus Christ our Lord." Romans 6:23. (Cf. John 3:36; 2 Timothy 1:1; 1 John 5:11.)

Furthermore, the Scriptures explicitly declare that "no murderer hath eternal life abiding in him" (1 John 3:15), and what is true of murderers is equally true of all unbelievers—they "shall not see [everlasting] life." (John 3:36. See context.)

Although God has given believers the assurance of eternal life here and now, He makes it abundantly clear that "this life is in his Son" (1 John 5:11); it is "hid with Christ in God" (Colossians 3:3). It is at the resurrection, not before, that "mortality" is "swallowed up of life." (Cf. 1 Corinthians 15:54; 2 Corinthians 5:4. See also John 6:39, 40, 54; 11:25, 26.) Until that time both believers and unbelievers are mortal.

Where Belief in Natural Immortality Came From

It is clear from the above Scripture passages, and others that might be cited, that the natural immortality of the soul or spirit is not taught in the Bible. Where did it come from? Robert McAfee Brown says in his *Handbook of Christian Theology* that the concept of the immortality of the soul "came into the stream of historic Christian faith chiefly through the Greek tributary."[1] Virtually all authorities in the field of church history agree with this conclusion.

The last enemy that shall be destroyed is death.

—1 Corinthians 15:26

Chapter 8

The Last Enemy

Egyptian Preoccupation With Death

Several years ago I had the privilege of accompanying a group that toured the Bible lands. One of the countries we visited was Egypt. If one thing impressed (perhaps I should say depressed) me more than anything else it was the ancient Egyptians' preoccupation with death. All the pyramids, mastabahs, and underground burial chambers depicted death and the afterworld. Some of the scenes showed the gods ferrying a *ka*, or soul, in a soul-boat to Osiris for judgment.

From reading translations from the *Book of the Dead,* it is evident that belief in the immortality of the soul permeated every aspect of Egyptian life. In fact, everyday life seemed to be one vast preparation for the afterlife in the spirit world.

The Hebrew Concept of Death

The Bible records that the Israelites sojourned in Egypt for several hundred years. (See Exodus 12:40, 41.) During this time they adopted many Egyptian customs, crafts, and concepts. For example, it is generally conceded that the newly liberated Hebrew slaves used Egyptian arts and crafts in the building of the tabernacle. But strangely enough, they did not incorporate into their theology the Egyptian belief that the soul is immortal.

The Bible Teaches That the Dead Are Unconscious

Instead of teaching the quasi-universal belief that the soul is immortal, the holy book of the Hebrews—the Old Testament—consistently teaches that man is unconscious in death. Here are a few Scripture passages that clearly set forth this view:

"In death there is no remembrance of thee: in the grave who shall give thee thanks?" Psalm 6:5. The latter part of this verse is a rhetorical question that demands a negative answer—the dead do not give thanks to God. This teaching is supported in the following Scripture passages:

"The dead praise not the Lord, neither any that go down into silence." Psalm 115:17.

"The grave cannot praise thee, death can not celebrate thee: they that go down into the pit cannot hope for thy truth." Isaiah 38:18.

"Oh that I had given up the ghost [*gava*, "expired"], and no eye had seen me! I should have been as though I had not been. . . . Let me alone, that I may take comfort a little, before I go whence I shall not return, even to the land of darkness and the shadow of death; a land of darkness, as darkness itself; and of the shadow of death, without any order, and where the light is as darkness." Job 10:18-22.

What more graphic description of the absolute oblivion of death could be given than this? But now notice this text:

"The living know that they shall die: but the dead know not any thing." Ecclesiastes 9:5.

This declaration by Solomon seems plain and is certainly in harmony with the rest of the teaching of Scripture on the nature of man.

(Additional Scripture passages speaking of the unconscious state of the dead may be found in Appendix D.)

What Happens at Death

According to the Bible, when a person dies "the dust return[s] to the earth as it was: and the spirit [*ruach*, the life-principle] . . . return[s] unto God who gave it." Ecclesiastes 12:7. This statement is a clear allusion to the record of Adam's creation and indicates that death is the opposite of creation.

Thus, if the formula for creation is: Body + life-principle = living soul with the potential for conscious existence, death must be the opposite of this: Body - life principle = dead soul without the potential for conscious existence. Is this what the Bible teaches? Let us see:

"While I live will I praise the Lord: I will sing praises unto my God while I have any being. Put not your trust in princes, nor in the son of man, in whom there is no help. His breath goeth forth, he returneth to his earth; in that very day his thoughts perish." Psalm 146:2-4.

The clear implication of verse 2 of Psalm 146 is that a time would come when the psalmist would no longer have any being. Verse 4 clearly implies that this time comes when the breath of life goes forth and a man returns to dust, that is, when he dies. The result of this is that "in that very day his thoughts perish." No being, no thought; no thought, no being. It is as simple as that.

From these and other Scripture passages that might be cited, it is clear that the Hebrew people—God's people in Old Testament times—believed that the dead were unconscious.

If the dead rise not, then is not Christ raised: and if Christ be not raised, your faith is vain; ye are yet in your sins. Then they also which are fallen asleep in Christ are perished

—1 Corinthians 15:16-18

Chapter 9

Resurrection

The Central Theme of the New Testament

Some years ago L. P. Jacks, editor of *British Quarterly Review*, declared that, after intensive study of the New Testament, he came to the following conclusion:

> The central theme of the New Testament, as it emerged before me in the course of this reading, is Immortality—not immortality of everybody, but of the believers in Christ as risen from the dead. This theme is found everywhere present, both in the Epistles and Gospels, either on the surface or beneath it; sometimes in the foreground with the light full on it (as in 1 Corinthians 15), sometimes in the middle distance, sometimes in the background; but its presence, whether in one position or another, always the unifying element, holding the parts together and making the New Testament a unitary whole. . . .
>
> This was my discovery of the New Testament as essentially and organically one, which it had never been to me before. Previously I had thought of it as a collection which would be more intelligible and more edifying if parts of it were removed—for instance if we had the Gospels, but not the Epistles, or only those parts of them which seemed to fit in with the Gospels. This I now saw to be a profound error. It seemed clear to me that all the parts are held together by the theme of the believer's immortality, so

that if this be withdrawn the whole disintegrates and falls asunder into fragments, many of great value but containing nothing to account for the origin of Christianity, and nothing on which the Christian Church could ever have been built. . . .

The whole of the New Testament seems to me covered, explained and held together by the saying "If Christ be not risen from the dead, then is our preaching vain."[1]

This is a remarkable conclusion, but is it valid? Apparently it is.

New Testament Emphasis

Because most of the Scripture passages that speak of man's constituent nature and his unconscious state in death are found in the Old Testament, some have concluded that the New Testament teaches a different doctrine concerning the nature of man than is taught in the Old Testament. Such a conclusion, however, is erroneous. The Bible is consistent. Both Testaments teach the same truth—*but from different viewpoints*. The Old Testament stresses man's mortality, whereas the New Testament emphasizes immortality—that life after death comes only through bodily resurrection.

What Resurrection Means

Both the Old and New Testaments describe resurrection as the reunion of the life-principle (*ruach*/*pneuma*) with the body which was dead. As a living soul came into conscious existence when God infused the breath of life into Adam's lifeless form, so when He reinfuses the breath of life into a dead body, it again becomes a living person capable of conscious existence. Here are a few biblical passages that teach this truth:

"The breath [*ruach*] came into them [the dead bodies in Ezekiel's vision of the valley of dry bones], and they lived, and stood up upon their feet, an exceeding great army." Ezekiel 37:10.

"If the Spirit [*pneuma*] of him that raised up Jesus from the dead dwell in you, he that raised up Christ from the dead shall also quicken [*zoopoieo*, literally, "make alive"] your mortal bodies by his Spirit [*pneuma*] that dwelleth in you." Romans 8:11.

"The people . . . shall not suffer their dead bodies to be put in graves. . . . And after three days and a half the spirit [*pnemua*] of life from God entered into them, and they stood upon their feet." Revelation 11:9-11.

It seems clear that the biblical formula for resurrection is similar, but not identical, to the formula for the original creation of the living soul. The formula for the original creation was: Lifeless body + breath of life = living soul. However, the resurrection formula is: Dead body + breath of life = individual, or soul, *restored* to life.

Observe that lifeless means that life is absent, whereas dead or death implies previous life. It is for this reason that in some instances the Bible speaks of the resurrection as the reunion of the *individual's* life-principle (*nephesh/psuche*) with his dead body, rather than simply the life-principle present in all living things (*ruach/pneuma*). For example:

"The soul [*nephesh*] of the child came into him again, and he revived." 1 Kings 17:22.

"Eutychus . . . was taken up dead. And Paul went down, and fell on him, and embracing him said, Trouble not yourselves; for his life [*psuche*] is in him." Acts 20:9, 10.

This seems to suggest that something happens to the life-principle during life which individualizes it. And yet it is still life-principle. So, it is not surprising that the Bible also uses *ruach/pneuma* in connection with resurrection. For instance, Luke 8:53-55 says:

"She [the daughter of Jairus] was dead. And he [Jesus] . . . took her by the hand, and called, saying, Maid arise. And her spirit [*pneuma*] came again, and she arose straightway." (See also Ezekiel 38:10; Romans 8:11; Revelation 11:9-11 quoted above.)

In those verses in which *nephesh/psuche* are used in connection with the resurrection, it seems to suggest that in some way the universal life-principle becomes individualized as a result of having been part of the living person. This does not mean that the life-principle has become a conscious entity. It does mean that *ruach/pneuma* have received the impress of individuality as the result of having been part of the living soul.

An Analogy

Perhaps an analogy at this point will be helpful. We call certain electromagnetic vibrations radio waves. Such waves have properties that distinguish them from other kinds of waves—ocean waves, for instance. When electromagnetic waves become "impressed" with, let us say, the human voice, they become "individualized," so to speak. Although their essential nature has not changed—they are still radio waves—yet they are different.

But there is something else to be considered: Even though these waves have become "individualized," their individuality does not become audible sound until they activate a radio receiver. Similarly, the individualized life-principle does not produce consciousness until it is recombined with the body at the resurrection. This, apparently, is what Paul is talking about, when he speaks of "our house which is from heaven" in 2 Corinthians 5:2. (See also verses 1, 3-6.)

Resurrection in the Bible

As Jacks points out, the theme of the resurrection as the fulfillment of the hope of God's people is a theme that runs like a golden thread throughout the New Testament. Glimpses of the same theme may also be seen in the Old Testament. Here are a few examples from both testaments:

"Thy dead men shall live, together with my dead body shall they arise. Awake and sing, ye that dwell in dust: for thy dew is as the dew of herbs, and the earth shall cast out the dead." Isaiah 26:19.

"Many of them that sleep in the dust of the earth shall awake, some to everlasting life, and some to shame and everlasting contempt." Daniel 12:2.

"Of all which . . . [the Father] hath given me [Christ] I should lose nothing, but should raise it up again at the last day." John 6:39. (Cf. verses 40, 44, and 54.)

"There shall be a resurrection of the dead, both of the just and unjust." Acts 24:15.

"We . . . groan within ourselves, waiting for the adoption, to wit, the redemption of our body." Romans 8:23.

(For other Scripture passages teaching the resurrection, see Appendix E.)

The Resurrection a Sine Qua Non

The New Testament clearly teaches that the resurrection is *positively essential* for there to be life after death. This does not mean that God could not have ordained that life after death could come by some other means, but it does mean that this is the way He has chosen to accomplish His purpose. The apostle Paul alludes to this essentiality of a bodily resurrection when he expresses the hope—"if by any means I might attain unto the resurrection of the dead." Philippians 3:11.

In 1 Corinthians 15 the apostle puts this teaching even more cogently in the following line of reasoning:

"If there be no resurrection of the dead, . . . then is not Christ raised: And if Christ be not raised, your faith is vain; ye are yet in your sins. *Then they also which are fallen asleep in Christ are perished.*" Verses 13-18. (Emphasis supplied.)

Ralph L. Keiper, paraphrasing these verses in the conservative, evangelical magazine *Eternity*, declares:

> If Christ did not rise from the dead, then our preaching is false, our faith is misguided, our witness is misleading, we have no salvation, there is no after life, we are still sinners, and we are hopelessly miserable. Paul seems to say, "Once you destroy the foundation—the resurrection of Christ—the superstructure is worthless."[2]

The biblical teaching, especially the New Testament teaching, concerning the afterlife seems clear and unequivocal: Without a bodily resurrection there is no life after death.

Is not my word like as a fire? saith the Lord; and like a hammer that breaketh the rock in pieces?

—Jeremiah 23:29

Chapter 10
"Hard Nuts" Cracked

Mistaken Identity

A few years ago a commuter train on the eastern seaboard of the United States collided with a freight train loaded with a flammable cargo, killing many passengers and starting an intense blaze that destroyed several coaches. After the fire was extinguished, coroners tried to identify the calcined remains of the dead. Some of these remains were identified as the bones of a businessman who regularly used the train and who, witnesses said, was on the train on the day of the disaster.

Hours later the man's family was notified of his death. They were, of course, shocked and grief-stricken. But what was their astonishment when the head of the house showed up at his front door after a night in the hospital, slightly injured but alive! For a moment they were sure they were seeing a ghost.

Someone had misidentified the man's bones!

A Human Error

We may be surprised that such a thing could happen, and yet is it really so surprising? After all, isn't it human to err? Of course it is.

But consider this. Many sincere Christians err in a manner similar to the way the coroners erred—when they *assume* that the Scriptures teach that the dead are conscious. The problem with such an assumption is that it makes the Bible contradict itself, and no one who believes that the Scriptures were inspired by God can accept that. "Let God be true, but every man

49

a liar." Romans 3:4. God, as will be shown, does not talk out of both sides of His mouth.

In this chapter and the next the major passages that are supposed to teach soul-survival will be examined and shown to be in harmony with the rest of the teaching of Scripture concerning man's nature.

The Souls Under the Altar

Some have thought that Revelation 6:9, 10 supports the teaching that the soul is conscious after death. The passage reads as follows:

"I saw under the altar the souls of them that were slain for the word of God. . . : And they cried with a loud voice, saying, How long, O Lord, holy and true, dost thou not judge and avenge our blood on them that dwell on the earth?"

To begin with, it must be remembered that much of the book of Revelation is written in symbolic language. Take, for example, the four horsemen of the Apocalypse. Simply reading their description makes it obvious that they are not literal but symbolic. Similarly, a reading of the description of the souls under the altar indicates that they too are symbolic. What, then, did the Revelator see and what did what he saw symbolize?

In Leviticus 17:14 blood stands for *nephesh* and in Numbers 6:6 *nephesh* denotes a dead body. Since Revelation draws largely on Old Testament imagery, what the Revelator probably saw was the slain bodies of Christian martyrs, their blood symbolically crying out for justice—*just as the blood of Abel symbolically cried out for justice.* (See Genesis 4:10.)

The Spirits in Prison

Some think that 1 Peter 3:18, 19 teaches that the spirit is conscious after death. These verses read as follows:

"Christ also hath once suffered for sins, the just for the unjust, that he might bring us to God, being put to death in the flesh, but quickened [*zoopoieo*, "made alive," i.e. resurrected] by the Spirit: by which also he went and preached unto the spirits in prison."

Were we to stop right here, there might be some justification for concluding that the Bible teaches that Christ preached the gospel to the spirits of the dead while He was in the grave—presumably to offer them a second chance at salvation. However, such a presumption would conflict with the plain scripture declaration that "they that go down into the pit [i.e. grave] cannot hope for thy truth." Isaiah 38:18.

But Peter continues in verse 20:

"Which [spirits] sometime were disobedient, when once the longsuffering of God waited in the days of Noah, while the ark was a preparing."

This verse identifies the spirits to whom Christ is alleged to have preached. They were the spirits of the antediluvians. Is it like Christ to favor a certain group with a second chance at salvation while presumably denying the same to others? Is Christ a respecter of persons? Of course not. (See Acts 10:34.) What, then, is the explanation?

Notice that Peter says that Christ was "quickened [i.e., made alive] by the Spirit." This could only be the Holy Spirit. (See Romans 8:11 for confirmation.) We conclude, therefore, that it was by or through the Holy Spirit, whose function it is to convict of sin (see John 16:8), that Christ "went and preached unto the [antediluvian] spirits in prison."

Did the Holy Spirit perform this function with respect to the antediluvians? He did. Genesis 6:3 quotes God as saying concerning these people, "My spirit [the Holy Spirit] shall not always strive with man."

Dr. B. H. Carroll, a former president of Southwestern Baptist Theological Seminary, and a believer in soul-survival, says:

> When He [Christ] preached to them [the spirits in prison], they were not disembodied. Christ preached through the Holy Spirit to the antediluvians while the ark was preparing, as Gen. 6:3 says, "My Spirit will not always strive with man." Through the Holy Spirit, Christ was preaching to those people while the ark was preparing. The very same Holy Spirit, when Christ's body died, made it alive in the resurrection. So in answering the question: "To whom did He preach?" I say that He preached to the antediluvians. When did He preach to

them? When they were disobedient in the days of Noah. How did He preach to them? By the Holy Spirit. Where are those people now? They are in prison shut up unto the judgment of the great day; they are dead now, and in the next chapter he [Peter] will say the gospel was preached to them that are dead for this cause [see 1 Peter 4:6]. They are dead now, but when they were living they had the gospel preached to them, but they rejected it.[1]

This explanation is reasonable. Peter is manifestly using *pneuma* here with reference to living people. This may seem an unusual use of *pneuma*, and yet, perhaps it is not so unusual after all, when one considers that conscience is simply another word for moral consciousness, and consciousness, as has been shown, is an invisible agent in living (not dead) human beings.

The Spirits of Just Men Made Perfect

Occasionally Hebrews 12:22, 23 is cited in support of the teaching that the spirit is immortal. These verses read as follows:

"Ye are come unto mount Sion, and unto the city of the living God, the heavenly Jerusalem, and to an innumerable company of angels, to the general assembly and church of the firstborn, . . . and to God the Judge of all, and to the spirits of just men made perfect."

In the first place Jesus speaks of born-again people who live in the flesh as being "spirit." (See John 3:6.) In so doing He obviously did not mean that one who is born again thereby becomes an invisible entity. He is speaking of living persons who have been given a new spiritual life through the new birth.

Dr. Adam Clarke, author of the famous Bible commentary bearing his name, and himself a believer in the immortality of the soul, had the correct idea, when he declared:

The spirits of just men made perfect, Heb. xii. 23, certainly means righteous men, and men still in the church militant.[2]

These spirits Hebrews 13 refers to were people still living in the flesh, not discarnate entities. Since *pneuma* in the New Testament is used to mean the new mind (an invisible agency, not entity) in a born-again individual (see John 3:6), this is apparently what the author of Hebrews intended. He simply used a part of the individual to represent the whole.

The Spirit Saved in the Day of the Lord Jesus

In 1 Corinthians 5:5 the apostle Paul instructs the church at Corinth to deal with an incestuous church member by delivering "such an one unto Satan for the destruction of the flesh, that the spirit may be saved in the day of the Lord Jesus." Some have thought that this passage somehow taught that the spirit was a conscious entity that is saved when Christ comes the second time. However, the Bible, as has been shown, plainly teaches that the resurrection means the "redemption of . . . [the] body." Romans 8:23. The Scriptures nowhere teach that those who are resurrected will be discarnate spirits in the hereafter. (Cf. Luke 24:36-43 with Philippians 3:20.)

How, then, is this text to be understood? Once again Paul is using *spirit* with the meaning of born-again person. What the apostle is saying is that by being excluded from church fellowship, and thus forfeiting divine protection, the offender would reap the cruel results of yielding to satanic control, and hopefully would experience the new birth—become spirit—and thus be saved when Christ comes the second time.

Departing to Be With Christ

Philippians 1:23 is sometimes cited as evidence that man is conscious in death. In this passage Paul says: "I am in a strait betwixt two, having a desire to depart, and to be with Christ; which is far better."

In the first place it should be pointed out that nowhere in this text or its context are the words *soul* or *spirit* used. The context surrounding this verse shows that Paul's chief concern is that Christ might be magnified.

When Paul wrote this epistle, he was a prisoner facing possible execution. It is for this reason that in verse 20 he says it is "my earnest expectation and my hope, that in nothing I shall be ashamed, but that with all boldness, as always, so now also Christ shall be magnified in my *body*, whether it be by life, or by death." (Emphasis supplied.)

As he weighs these two alternatives (life and death), Paul sees that a continuation of his life will glorify Christ—souls will be saved by his labors. But death also has its advantages. If he is martyred, Christ will also be glorified—souls will be saved by his martyrdom. So, the great apostle finds himself "in a strait, betwixt two" (verse 23), *and by two he obviously means life and death.*

Now, if "to depart, and to be with Christ; which is far better," means death, as some claim, Paul would have faced no dilemma whatever. He would have chosen death. But he doesn't. Why? Because there is a third alternative which "is far better." What is this alternative? It is the only alternative left—translation to heaven without seeing death. This is what happened to Enoch and Elijah. (See Hebrews 11:5; 2 Kings 2:11; Matthew 17:3.) This is what will happen to the living saints at the second coming.

Now, while translation was the "far better" alternative Paul would have chosen, he goes on to say, "Nevertheless to abide in the flesh is more needful for you [Philippians]." Verse 24. Paul realized that while death would bring him rest and translation would usher him immediately into Christ's presence, continuing to live and witness for Christ was more needful for the Philippian Christians. So, Philippians 1:23 does not teach consciousness in death after all.

In the next chapter two other common objections will be dealt with—Saul and the witch of Endor, and the Rich Man and Lazarus.

Wise souls are going, like King Saul of old, to those who have familiar spirits . . . that they may receive consolation and instruction in times of great unrest.
—Albert E. Vaughn Strode in *The National Spiritualist,* July 1951.
(Emphasis supplied.)

Chapter 11

More Nuts Cracked

Sometimes hard questions have simple answers. This is the case with the story of King Saul's night visit to the witch of Endor, as well as the parable of the Rich Man and Lazarus. These passages are frequently cited as evidence for soul-survival. The record of Saul's visit to the witch's abode reads as follows:

Saul and the Witch of Endor

"Now Samuel was dead, and all Israel had lamented him, and buried him in Ramah, even in his own city. And Saul had put away those that had familiar spirits, and the wizards, out of the land. And the Philistines gathered themselves together, and came and pitched in Shunem: and Saul gathered all Israel together, and they pitched in Gilboa. And when Saul saw the host of the Philistines, he was afraid, and his heart greatly trembled. And when Saul enquired of the Lord, the Lord answered him not, neither by dreams, nor by Urim, nor by prophets.

"Then said Saul unto his servants, Seek me a woman that hath a familiar spirit, that I may go to her, and enquire of her.

"And his servants said to him, Behold, there is a woman that hath a familiar spirit at Endor.

"And Saul disguised himself, and put on other raiment, and he went, and two men with him, and they came to the woman by night: and he said, I pray thee, divine unto me by the familiar spirit, and bring me him up, whom I shall name unto thee.

"And the woman said unto him, Behold, thou knowest what Saul hath done, how he hath cut off those that have familiar spirits, and the wizards, out of the land: wherefore then layest thou a snare for my life, to cause me to die?

"And Saul sware to her by the Lord, saying, As the Lord liveth, there shall no punishment happen to thee for this thing.

"Then said the woman, Whom shall I bring up unto thee?

"And he said, Bring me up Samuel.

"And when the woman saw Samuel, she cried with a loud voice: and the woman spake unto Saul, saying, Why hast thou deceived me? for thou art Saul.

"And the king said unto her, Be not afraid: for what sawest thou?

"And the woman said unto Saul, I saw gods ascending out of the earth.

"And he said unto her, What form is he of?

"And she said, An old man cometh up; and he is covered with a mantle.

"And Saul perceived that it was Samuel, and he stooped with his face to the ground, and bowed himself.

"And Samuel said to Saul, Why hast thou disquieted me, to bring me up?

"And Saul answered, I am sore distressed; for the Philistines make war against me, and God is departed from me, and answereth me no more, neither by prophets, nor by dreams: therefore I have called thee, that thou mayest make known unto me what I shall do.

"Then said Samuel, Wherefore then dost thou ask of me, seeing the Lord is departed from thee, and is become thine enemy? And the Lord hath done to him, as he spake by me: for the Lord hath rent the kingdom out of thine hand, and given it to thy neighbor, even to David: Because thou obeyedst not the voice of the Lord, nor executedst his fierce wrath upon Amalek, therefore hath the Lord done this thing unto thee this day. Moreover the Lord will also deliver Israel with thee into the hand of the Philistines: and to morrow shalt thou and thy sons be with me." 1 Samuel 28:3-19.

Erroneous Conclusion

Because the entity who appeared to the witch and spoke to Saul is called Samuel, some have assumed that it was actually God's prophet Samuel. In his otherwise excellent book *Occult ABC*, Kurt E. Koch reflects this view, when he says:

> An unexpected turn is clearly seen in this Bible narrative. The medium would probably have deceived the disguised king Saul, as she had deceived many others over the years. But suddenly she cried out. God had stepped in and taken over. Samuel appeared, sent by God to pronounce the death sentence on King Saul.[1]

A Better Answer

In the first place, is it like God to work hand in glove with an agent of His archenemy? No, it is not. What, then, is the answer?

First Samuel 28:6 says, "Saul enquired of the Lord," but 1 Chronicles 10:14 says that the disobedient king "enquired not of the Lord." Is this a contradiction? No, only a paradox. Saul "enquired of the Lord" when he consulted "dreams" and "Urim" and "prophets," but when he consulted the witch of Endor, "he enquired not of the Lord." Therefore he must have been consulting the witch's familiar spirit.

First Samuel 28:15 supports this explanation. When Saul said, "God is departed from me, and answereth me no more, neither by prophets, nor by dreams: *therefore I have called thee*," it is obvious that God was not answering the disobedient king—*and he knew it!* This conclusion is incontrovertibly confirmed by the fact that 1 Chronicles 10:13 plainly says that "Saul died . . . for asking counsel of one that had a familiar spirit, *to enquire of it*." The one who spoke to Saul was not Samuel, but the witch's "familiar spirit" impersonating Samuel.

But, if this is true, why does 1 Samuel 28 call the familiar spirit Samuel? The Bible is simply using the language of appearance. This is not unusual. We say the sun travels from east to west, because it *appears* to do so. In actual fact, the sun stands still while the earth rotates from west to east, making it *appear* to do the opposite.

The Rich Man and Lazarus

Another objection that is frequently raised is the story of the Rich Man and Lazarus. The story reads as follows:

"There was a certain rich man, which was clothed in purple and fine linen, and fared sumptuously every day: and there was a certain beggar named Lazarus, which was laid at his gate full of sores, and desiring to be fed with the crumbs which fell from the rich man's table: moreover the dogs came and licked his sores.

"And it came to pass, that the beggar died, and was carried by the angels into Abraham's bosom: the rich man also died, and was buried; and in hell [Gr.*hades*] he lifted up his eyes, being in torments, and seeth Abraham afar off, and Lazarus in his bosom. And he cried and said, Father Abraham, have mercy on me, and send Lazarus, that he may dip the tip of his finger in water, and cool my tongue; for I am tormented in this flame.

"But Abraham said, Son, remember that thou in thy lifetime receivedst thy good things, and likewise Lazarus evil things: but now he is comforted, and thou art tormented. And besides all this, between us and you there is a great gulf fixed: so that they which would pass from hence to you cannot; neither can they pass to us, that would come from thence.

"Then he said, I pray thee therefore, father, that thou wouldest send him to my father's house: for I have five brethren; that he may testify unto them, lest they also come into this place of torment.

"Abraham saith unto him, They have Moses and the prophets; let them hear them.

"And he said, Nay, father Abraham: but if one went unto them from the dead, they will repent.

"And he said unto them, If they hear not Moses and the prophets, neither will they be persuaded, though one rose from the dead." Luke 16:19-31.

The point of this narrative is stated in the last verse just quoted. So, the first question to be asked is: Who were "they" Jesus was alluding to? Verse 14 tells us. "The Pharisees . . . , who were covetous, heard all these things [the preceding parables]: and they derided him." Since Jesus was directing this story at this group, the next question is: What did the Pharisees believe about life after death?

The Pharisees and Life After Death

The Jewish historian Flavius Josephus, a near contemporary of Jesus and himself a Pharisee, tells us. In his "Discourse Concerning Hades," he says:

Hades is a place in the world not regularly finished; a *subterranean* region, where the light of this world does not shine. . . . This region is allowed as a place of custody for souls, which angels are appointed as guardians to them, who distribute them *temporary punishment*, agreeable to everyone's behavior and manners.

In this region there is a certain place set apart, as *a lake of unquenchable fire*, wherein we suppose no one hath hitherto been cast; but it is prepared for a day aforedetermined by God, in which one righteous sentence shall deservedly be passed upon all men; when the unjust and those who have been disobedient to God . . . shall be adjudged to this *everlasting punishment*, . . . while the just shall obtain *an incorruptible* and never-fading *kingdom*. These are now indeed confined in Hades, but not in the same place wherein the unjust are confined.

For there is one descent into this region, at whose *gate* we believe there stands an archangel with an host; which *gate* when those pass through that are conducted down by the angels appointed over souls, they do not go the same way; but the just are guided to the *right hand*, and are led with hymns sung by the *angels* appointed over that place, unto a region of *light*, in which the just have dwelt from the beginning of the world. . . . This place we call The Bosom of Abraham.

But as to the unjust, they are dragged by force to the

left hand, by the angels allotted for punishment. . . . Now those angels that are set over these souls, drag them into the neighborhood of hell itself; who, when they are hard by it, continually hear the noise of it, and do not stand clear of the hot vapour; but when they have a nearer view of this spectacle, as a terrible and exceeding great prospect of fire, they are struck with fearful expectation of a future judgment, and in effect punished thereby; and not only so, but where they see the place [or choir] of the *fathers* and of the just, even hereby are they punished; for a *chaos* deep and large is fixed between them; insomuch that a just man that hath compassion upon them, cannot be admitted, nor can one that is unjust, if he were bold enough to attempt it, pass over it."[2] (Emphasis Whiston's.)

Why Jesus Told This Parable

In the light of Josephus's statement it seems clear that Jesus told the parable of the Rich Man and Lazarus simply to show that the Pharisees were condemned by their own erroneous beliefs. This was a tactic Jesus frequently used to turn tables on His enemies. (See Matthew 21:23-46; 22:1-46.) But the use of this tactic in no way establishes that Jesus held the Pharisee's unscriptural belief that the dead are conscious and that heaven and hell are within shouting distance of each other.

Other lesser objections must be passed over because of space limitations.

Our contest is not with human foes alone, but with the rulers, authorities, and cosmic powers of this dark world; that is, with the spirit-forces of evil challenging us in the heavenly contest.
—Ephesians 6:12, C. B. Williams translation

Chapter 12
The Unseen War

A Spirit Reveals His True Identity

Some years ago a woman living in the San Francisco Bay area, who will simply be identified as Edna, was told that she had a natural talent for channeling. Soon after this she began developing her abilities as a writing medium. Every morning she would go into a room, pull down the blinds, sit with pencil and paper in hand, and wait. Eventually an unseen power would grip her wrist, and her hand would begin to move.

Although she was no artist, while under spirit control Edna could draw almost anything, usually flowers. As her powers grew, she began to write messages. Meanwhile she prayed that if this were a good power, God would help her use it to His glory, and if not, that He would show her clearly that it was evil.

One morning Edna drew a picture that looked like nothing she had ever seen before. She looked at it for a long time before asking her spirit guide what it was. Her hand began to write. The following quotation is substantially what the invisible intelligence wrote:

This represents the devil. I am not one of your departed friends as you have thought. You are praying for light. If you stick with this [i.e. channeling], you will become a wonderful medium, one of the world's best. If you give it up and stick to the Bible and serve God, you will have misery untold. You will get along nicely for a time; then you will begin to go down, until everything you have is taken from you. Then if you still persist, your little girl will be taken from you. But if you will give up prayer and your Bible, you may become a noted medium, and will have wonderful power and great wealth.

The spirit, still holding Edna's wrist, paused, apparently waiting for her decision. After a long time, she didn't know how long, she laughed out loud. "How foolish!" she thought. "How could this be the devil? Why should he reveal himself this way?" At this the spirit gave her arm such a painful twist that she winced. Soon her hand began to move again. This is what it wrote:

I have told you the truth. Now is the time for you to decide. You must choose either to worship God, or to become a medium. And you had better not laugh. You will see in time that what I have said is true.

I am happy to tell you that Edna chose to serve God even though it meant hardships for her.[1]

Did the Spirit Tell the Truth?

Earlier it was stated that it is impossible to establish with deception-proof certainty the true identity of beings that exist outside our world of experience. However, it seems that in this case a lying spirit told the truth—at least in part. Why? I believe it was because God compelled him to do so. But why? Apparently because (1) Edna truly did not know whom she was dealing with, and (2) she was sincerely seeking for truth. As a consequence God honored her prayer.

But just because a spirit told the truth in Edna's case does not mean that God will always compel the spirits to tell the truth or reveal their true identity. Much seems to depend on the extent of one's knowledge of Bible truth and the degree of one's sincerity—*something only God can determine.* Anyone who thinks he can identify spirits apart from the power of God and His Word is presumptuous and lays himself open to deception.

How It All Began

The Bible plainly teaches that behind the scenes of earthly affairs a titanic struggle is going on between the forces of good and evil. (See Ephesians 6:12, quoted earlier.) This battle is being waged for the control of minds. Concerning this conflict, Revelation 12:7-9 says:

"There was war in heaven: Michael and his angels fought against the dragon; and the dragon fought and his angels, and prevailed not; neither was their place found any more in heaven. And the great dragon was cast out, that old serpent, called the Devil, and Satan, which deceiveth the whole world: he was cast out into the earth, and his angels were cast out with him."

This is how it all began. Sin originated in heaven, and it involved angels.

According to the Bible, angels are created beings (see Psalm 148:2-5). They are called spirits (see Psalm 104:1-6)—invisible agents. These invisible entities are by nature superior to human beings in intelligence and power. (See Psalm 8:4, 5; 2 Peter 2:10, 11; 2 Samuel 14:20.)

The Old Serpent in the Garden of Eden

The identification of Satan, the leader of the fallen angels in Revelation 12, as "that old serpent" clearly points to the story of the fall recorded in Genesis 3:1-6, where a seemingly harmless snake tempted Eve to disobey God. Here is what Genesis says:

"Now the serpent was more subtil than any beast of the field which the Lord God had made. And he said unto the woman, Yea, hath God said, Ye shall not eat of every tree of the garden?

"And the woman said unto the serpent, We may eat of the fruit of the trees of the garden: but of the fruit of the tree which is in the midst of the garden, God hath said, Ye shall not eat of it, neither shall ye touch it, lest ye die.

"And the serpent said unto the woman, Ye shall not surely die: for God doth know that in the day ye eat thereof, then your eyes shall be opened, and ye shall be as gods, knowing good and evil.

"And when the woman saw that the tree was good for food,

and that it was pleasant to the eyes, and a tree to be desired to make one wise, she took of the fruit thereof, and did eat, and gave also unto her husband with her; and he did eat."

In Ezekiel 28:12-19, under the figure of the king of Tyrus, a "cherub" (an angelic being), created "perfect" in whom was found "iniquity," is said to have been "in Eden the garden of God." This angel is described as being "full of wisdom" (verses 15, 12), but it says he fell because his "heart was lifted up" (verse 17). Isaiah 14:12-14 says that he aspired to be "like the most High."

Angels Invisible to Humans Before the Fall

"Cast out into the earth" with those "angels which kept not their first estate" (Revelation 12:9 and Jude 6; see also Luke 10:18), this being deceived Adam and Eve either by using a serpent as a channel or by appearing in the guise of a serpent.

In either case it is evident that even before the fall angels were invisible to human eyes, for Eve did not see the invisible agent that deceived her. Furthermore, it is evident that the master deluder knew he possessed this power. Having introduced sin and death into the world, is it any wonder that he and his angels, who can transform themselves into angels of light and ministers of righteousness (see 2 Corinthians 11:14, 15) can also impersonate the dead in order to give the first lie a semblance of truth?

In his conversation with Eve, the great deceiver promised two things: (1) That she and her husband would not die, as God had warned, and (2) that they would be as "gods."

Let us take the second promise first—"ye shall be as gods."

Ye Shall Be *As Elohim*

When Satan promised Eve, "Ye shall be as gods [*elohim*]," he seems to have purposely used a word that has a variety of meanings. *Elohim* is usually rendered "God" or "gods," but it may also be translated "judges," as in Exodus 21:6 and 22:8, 9, and there are reasons to believe that in 1 Samuel 28:13 it should be translated "judge."

The reason for this is that when the witch of Endor said, "I saw gods [*elohim*] ascending out of the earth," Saul understood her to be using *elohim* in the singular, for in the very next verse he asked, "What form is *he* of?" The fact that Samuel was a judge (see 1 Samuel 7:6) makes it almost certain that *elohim* should be translated "judge" in this instance.

Thus, by telling Eve that by eating of the forbidden fruit she would become as *elohim*, the great deluder could be understood to mean, "You will be a judge, knowing good and evil," or, "You will be gods, knowing good and evil," or even, "You will be God, knowing good and evil." Such ambiguity is characteristic of the "old serpent." He used it in ancient times, and he still uses it today.

You Are God!

The concept that in one way or another man is God is being accepted by increasing numbers of people in the United States and foreign countries. For instance, in her book *Out on a Limb*, Miss MacLaine quotes a spirit who identifies himself as "John," as saying, "You are God."[2]

In Miss MacLaine's book *It's All in the Playing,* movie producer Stan Margulies quotes the actress as shouting " 'I am God,' " and informs her that three people who heard her make this declaration said they thought God was punishing the actors and movie makers because of this assertion.

Miss MacLaine does not disavow this claim. Instead she reaffirms it without apology and encourages others to do likewise. Thus she writes:

> Was God punishing me for blasphemy? No, I think he would want each one of us to recognize the God within ourselves and take responsibility for that immediately; to recognize each person as divine. Each person was God. I thought God would have loved that scene. To say, "I am God" was to fulfill and respect his love for us, because we were all part of that divinity.[3]

Most Christians recognize this claim for what it is—an echo of the serpent's first falsehood. Thus, in their book *The Seduction of Christianity*, Dave Hunt and T. A. McMahon warn:

The new world religion of Antichrist . . . will promise to lead humanity into the experience of its own divinity, *that each of us is "God."* This basic lie of the serpent in the Garden of Eden will seem to be validated by the godlike psychic powers the Antichrist will manifest and the whole world will pursue.[4] (Emphasis supplied.)

These authors go on to say:

Werner Erhard, founder of est (Erhard Seminars Training), declares, "You're god in your universe." Creme's Maitreya states, "Man is an emerging God. . . . My plan and My Duty is to reveal to you a new way . . . which will permit the divine in man to shine forth." Maharishi Mahesh Yogi, founder of the TM cult, perverts the Bible by saying, "Be still and know that you are God. . . ." Sun Myung Moon has written, "God and man are one. Man is incarnate God." Echoing the same lie from Eden's serpent, Ernest Holmes, founder of the Church of Religious Science, declared, "All men are spiritually evolving until . . . each will fully express his divinity."[5]

Ye Shall Not Surely Die

Although most Christians would agree with Hunt and McMahon, it should be pointed out that these authors and other Christian writers fail to point out the other part of Satan's original falsehood—"ye shall not surely die."

The belief that a person is conscious after death opens the door "to seducing spirits" and attempted communication with the dead. It is for this reason that God warns His people again and again against dealing with those who have "familiar spirits." (See Leviticus 19:31; 20:6, 27; Deuteronomy 18:11; 1 Samuel 28:3, 9; 2 Kings 21:6; 23:24; 1 Chronicles 10:13; 2 Chronicles 33:6; Isaiah 8:19, 20; 19:3, where *ob* is used.)

A Deathbed Vision

In his book *The Evidences of Immortality*, evangelical writer Harry Rimmer reports on a deathbed vision, recounting what a dying young woman's mother, aunt, and a nurse said they saw just before she expired:

> In the place of the hospital walls, they clearly saw a garden. Coming down the path of this garden, with a smile on her face and hands extended in greeting, they saw the form of the grandmother who had gone to be with the Lord more than a year before. They heard the dying girl laugh, and glancing at her they saw a smile of delight upon her face. She nodded on her pillow, and with a smile of happiness fixed in place, her spirit fled her body. The nurse and the other women hastened to her side, and when they thought to look back at the corner of the room where the vision had been, nothing was there but the plain walls of the hospital room. Evidence of this type is supplementary, but it is highly suggestive. None of the witnesses of this event are of the emotional or hysterical type. This experience could be multiplied by able testimony of the same nature from many sources. While such evidence is only suggestive, *it is at least light through the lattice.* Such glimpses over the border of the world that now is, into the one that then shall be, *may be advanced proof of immortality, for the comfort of those who really dwell on the borderland of the supernatural.*[6] (Emphasis supplied.)

Spontaneous Visions of the Dead

With all due respect for the author just quoted, who is obviously a sincere Christian and an opponent of attempted spirit communication, those who entertain the notion that spontaneous visitations of the dead are special dispensations of Providence sent to comfort the bereaved lay themselves open to satanic deceptions. Some who have taken this position have in their grief been led to attempt to communicate with the supposed spirits of their dead loved ones, only to be ensnared by "the spirits of devils, working miracles." Revelation 16:14.

God's dealings are consistent with His Word. He does not say one thing and do another. The mingling of good and evil is Satan's method of operation, not God's. "Let God be true, but every man a liar." Romans 3:4.

If the father of lies or one of his evil angels appears to promote truth and righteousness, we may be sure that their ultimate aim is to deceive. Clearly, there is no concord between Christ and Belial. (See 2 Corinthians 6:14, 15.) God does not work hand in glove with the devil.

God's counsel to His people is: "When they say to you, 'Seek those who are mediums and wizards, who whisper and mutter,' should not a people seek their God? Should they seek the dead on behalf of the living? To the law and to the testimony! If they do not speak according to this word, it is because there is no light in them." Isaiah 8:19, 20, NKJV.

The law and the testimony are another name for the Bible. Elsewhere in Scripture the Bible describes itself as a sword. Against this Sword the invisible forces of evil are powerless. (See Ephesians 6:17.)

They are the spirits of devils, working miracles.

—Revelation 16:14

Chapter 13

Catching the Spirit

The Schmidts and the Ticking Sounds

In an earlier chapter I related an experience Bill and Helen Schmidt told me about when her son was killed in the Indianapolis 500. During a subsequent visit they told me about another incident that took place a short time after Franny lost his life.

Besides Franny, Helen had another son, Robert, who was an airplane pilot. Within months of Franny's death Bob was killed in a plane crash. Soon after his funeral the Schmidts began hearing light ticking noises in their home. At first they attributed them to mice, but as the days passed the ticking became louder and more insistent. The sounds appeared to come from between one of the bedroom walls. But when Bill removed the sheetrock from the wall, he found nothing, and no sooner had the drywall been removed, than the noises began coming from the other side of the room. That did it. The Schmidts decided to move.

At the time this was happening Bill and Helen were living in the Los Angeles area. They decided to move to Paradise in northern California to get away from the annoying disturbances. Helen drove to Paradise with Bob's four-year-old son, Bobby, to househunt. After spending almost the entire day looking, she found a house she liked. By now the sun had set, and the landlord graciously offered to let her and Bobby spend the night in the partially furnished house. Helen accepted the offer.

As soon as she retired, Helen began hearing those terrible ticking sounds again, only this time they were more insistent than ever. Finally in desperation she spoke out loud and said, "I don't know what this means, but if it's something I need to know, speak out or give me a dream."

Immediately the ticking stopped, and she fell asleep. She dreamed she was strolling down a sidewalk holding Bobby by the hand. On her right was a low stone wall on the top of which was a wrought-iron fence. Beyond the grating stood a magnificent stone mansion on a slight elevation surrounded by a beautiful green lawn and graceful trees. Helen had never before seen the place, and yet somehow it seemed familiar.

After a bit she and Bobby came to an iron gate. Helen opened it, and the two trudged up a flagstone walk and onto the porch of the mansion. She knocked, the door opened, and a tall, pleasant-looking young man in a black suit let them in. It was then that Helen heard a man sobbing uncontrollably somewhere upstairs.

The man in the black suit led her and Bobby up a staircase toward the sound of the weeping. At the top of the stairs and to her left a door led into a large room. In the room seated on a couch Helen saw Bob. His face was buried in his hands, and he was crying as if his heart would break. He kept repeating over and over, "Oh, if I could just live my life over again, I would live differently."

Helen sat down next to Bob and tried to comfort him. In the meantime Bobby walked around a coffee table in front of the couch and stood there staring at his father, a look of wonderment on his face. After a while the weeping subsided, and Bob reached into a candy bowl on the coffee table and handed a chocolate to Bobby. Helen protested that Bobby had already eaten too much candy for one day, but Bob gave him the chocolate anyway.

Meanwhile, from a music album perched on a shelf, the man in the black suit took a record, set it on a record player, and the most beautiful music Helen had ever heard poured forth. As the music played, Helen continued to converse with her son. He was seated on her left. All of a sudden he wasn't there anymore. She looked around and discovered he was now sitting on her right.

After a while the man in the black suit nodded, and Helen understood that the visit was over. She rose to leave, bade Bob goodbye, and, accompanied by Bobby, followed the man in the black suit down the stairs. As she walked out of the house and onto the porch the door closed, and everything suddenly turned to noise and confusion. She woke up with a start.

The Power of Jesus' Name

While Helen was relating her experience, I began hearing a sharp ticking sound in the ceiling of the room in which we were sitting. Helen, I learned later, didn't hear it. I wondered whether or not Bill heard it. I glanced in his direction, and he responded by looking up toward the source of the sound and nodding his head, as if to say, "That's it, all right."

Without disturbing the narrative, I prayed silently. My petition went something like this: "Dear God, I claim the promise of 1 John 1:9 ('If we confess our sins, he is faithful and just to forgive us our sins, and to cleanse us from all unrighteousness.'). I know You are infinitely powerful, and You can stop that ticking sound. If it can bring glory to Your name, please make it stop right now, in Jesus' name. Amen."

The ticking stopped instantly—and permanently! When Helen finished her story, we told her what had just happened. Then we prayed and thanked God for the manifestation of His power.

Words of Caution

Anyone who presumes to deal with invisible intelligences on his own terms is susceptible to their deceptions. Fraud is the stock and trade of lying spirits—*even when they appear to be doing good or to be telling the truth!*

These agents of evil seem not to care whether they practice the deception, whether it is practiced by the channeler, or whether it is practiced by the observer. It all suits their nefarious purpose. Is it any wonder that it is generally recognized that the occult is laced with fraud?

Only those who love Bible truth and live up to the light shining on them from God's Word are safe from Satan's wicked machinations.

The Spirit That Got Caught

Many years ago a Mr. William B. Lanning of Trenton, New Jersey, attended a series of séances. After a while he became suspicious that the messages coming through the writing medium were not originating with the dead relatives they purported to come from. During his last sitting he determined with God's help to discover the identity of these entities that purported to be his dead loved ones. Afterwards Mr. J. W. Daniels, a friend of Mr. Lanning, wrote the following account, apparently based on the automatic writing left by the spirit.

> The spirit on being asked if it was right and beneficial for the human race to consult these spirits, replied, "Yes, it will make them happier and better." He then testified in substance to the main doctrines of these spirits, and said that though he died an unconverted man he was happy—that departed Christians were among these spirits—all of them were happy—there was to be no resurrection of the dead, no future punishment, nor any day of judgment.
>
> On being cross-examined a little, the spirit became angry and unwilling to answer, and begged to depart— said he would go and get more spirits and return. Said my friend, "No. When you go I want you to stay away; but at the present do you answer my questions. *In the name of the Lord I demand it.*"
>
> The "happy" spirit quailed, and Mr. L[anning] proceeded:
>
> Is the Bible true[?] Yes.
>
> The Bible forbids necromancy and the consulting of familiar spirits. Which shall I believe, you or the Bible? The Bible.
>
> Why did you tell me that it was right and useful to consult the spirits? Because I wanted to deceive you.

What is the business of these spirits with men? What do you think it is?

I think it is to deceive. Very well, you are correct.

Are you happy[?] No. I am miserable.

Is there a hell? Yes.

Are you in hell? No, not yet.

Do you expect to go there? Yes.

When? At the day of judgment.

Is there to be a day of judgment? Yes.

Have you any prospect of happiness? I HAVE NO HOPE!

In the name of the Lord, is there a good spirit—the spirit of a departed Christian among all these rapping and writing spirits? *No, not one.*

Where are the spirits of the departed Christians? THE LORD HAS TAKEN THEM.

Why then did you tell my brother in Philadelphia the contrary of all this? Because I wished to deceive him.

Could you deceive him[?] Yes.

[The brother was a spiritualist.] (*sic*)

Why could you deceive him? Because he is a fool.

Can't you deceive me? No.

Why? Because you believe the Bible.

Will you tell my brother what you have told me? Yes.

I want to hear from you no more; good-bye forever. *Spirit.*—Good-bye forever.[1] (All emphases his.)

Conclusion

The foregoing confrontation reveals that manifestations purporting to be the souls or spirits of the dead are deceptions palmed off by the spirits of devils. Such manifestations, whether sought or unsought, are nothing less than the most shameless fraud ever perpetrated in the name of life's tenderest memories.

The Bible warns that in the last days the great deceiver's strategies will increase in subtlety, for he knows he has but a short time. (See Matthew 24:24; Revelation 12:12.) If Satan and his evil angels have the ability to transform themselves into angels of light and ministers of righteousness (see 2 Corinthians 11:14, 15), why should it be thought impossible for them to also impersonate our dead loved ones?

How to Escape Satan's Latter-Day Delusions

Unaided by divine power, human beings cannot hope to escape Satan's latter-day deceptions, for these evil agencies will deceive, if possible, the very elect. (See Matthew 24:24.)

Although Satan and his angels are defeated foes, human beings in their own strength are no match for them. This means that although a Christian need not fear evil spirits, neither will he presumptuously confront them or trifle with them.

Christians need to remember that the only way they can prevail over these enemies of righteousness is the way Jesus triumphed over them in the wilderness of temptation. His appeal to the Word of God—"it is written"—routed the archdeceiver. (See Matthew 4:1-11; Luke 4:1-13.) By this same Word, fortified by the power of Christ, we, too, can come off more than conquerors! The Bible says: "They overcame him [Satan] by the blood of the Lamb, and by the word of their testimony." Revelation 12:11.

Appendix A

Nephesh

I. *Nephesh* is used of *man* as an individual person in 53 passages and rendered in six different ways. Typical examples in parentheses accompany some references:
   1. *soul(s)*—Gen. 2:7; 12:5; 46:15, 18, 22, 25, 26 (twice), 27. Ex. 1:5; 12:4. Lev. 22:11. 1 Sam. 18:1. Ps. 25:20. Prov. 10:3; 11:25, 30; 14:25; 19:15; 22:23; 25:25; 27:7 (twice). Jer. 38:16. Lam. 3:25. Ezek. 13:18, 19, 20 (three times); 18:4 (three times).
   2. *person(s)*—Gen. 14:21; 36:6. Ex. 16:16. Lev. 27:2. Num. 19:18; 31:35, 40 (twice), 46. Deut. 10:22. Jer. 43:6; 52:29, 30 (twice). Ezek. 16:5; 27:13.
   3. *any*—Lev. 24:17. Deut. 24:7.
   4. *man*—2 Kings 12:4.
   5. Not rendered by the KJV translators (Num. 31:35; 1 Chron. 5:21).
II. *Nephesh* is used of *man* as exercising certain powers or performing certain acts (and as such may properly be translated by a pronoun) in 96 passages, with eleven renderings:
   1. *soul(s)*—Gen. 27:4, 19, 25, 31. Lev. 4:2; 5:1, 2, 4, 15, 17; 6:2; 7:18, 20, 21, 27; 16:29, 31; 17:12, 15; 20:6, 25; 22:6; 23:27, 30, 32. Num. 15:27, 28, 30 (twice); 19:22; 29:7; 30:2, 4 (twice), 5, 6, 7, 8, 9, 10, 11, 12, 13. Deut. 13:6. Judg. 5:21. 1 Sam. 1:26; 17:55; 18:3; 20:3, 17; 25:26. 2 Sam. 11:11;

14:19. 2 Kings 2:2, 4, 6; 4:30. Job 16:4 (twice); 31:30. Ps. 35:13; 120:6. Prov. 6:32; 8:36; 11:17; 13:2; 15:32; 16:17; 19:8, 16; 20:2; 21:23; 22:5; 29:24. Eccl. 4:8; 6:2. Isa. 51:23; 58:3. Jer. 4:19; 6:8 [of God]; 9:9 [of God]. Ezek. 4:14. Mic. 6:7.
2. *man*—Ex. 12:16.
3. *any*—Lev. 2:1.
4. *one*—Lev. 4:27.
5. *yourselves*—Lev. 11:43, 44. Jer. 17:21.
6. *person*—Num. 5:6.
7. *themselves*—Esther 9:31. Isa. 46:2.
8. *himself*—Job 18:4; 32:2.
9. *he*—Ps. 105:18.
10. *herself*—Jer. 3:11.
11. *Himself*—Jer. 51:14. Amos 6:8. (Used in reference to God.)

III. *Nephesh* is used of *man* as possessing animal appetites and desires in 22 passages rendered in five different ways:
1. *soul(s)*—Num. 11:6 (dried away), 21:5 (loatheth). Deut. 12:15 (lusteth), 20 (longeth to eat flesh), 20 (lusteth after), 21 (lusteth); 14:26 (lusteth), 26 (desireth). 1 Sam. 2:16 (desireth). Job 6:7 (refused); 33:20 (abhorreth). Ps. 107:18 (abhorreth). Prov. 6:30 (hungry); 13:25 (satisfying). Isa. 29:8 (empty), 8 (hath appetite). Mic. 7:1 (desired fruit).
2. *pleasure*—Deut. 23:24.
3. *lust*—Ps. 78:18.
4. *appetite*—Prov. 23:2. Eccl. 6:7.
5. *greedy*—Isa. 56:11.

IV. *Nephesh* is used of *man* as exercising mental faculties, and manifesting certain feelings and affections and passions in 231 passages and rendered in twenty different ways:
1. *soul(s)*—Gen. 34:3 (clave), 8 (longeth); 42:21 (anguish); 49:6 (cometh not). Lev. 26:11 (not abhor), 15 (abhor), 30 (abhor), 43 (abhorred). Num. 21:4 (discouraged). Deut. 4:9 (keep), 29

(seek); 6:5 (love); 10:12 (serve); 11:13 (love), 18 (lay up in); 13:3 (love); 26:16 (keep); 30:2 (return), 6 (love), 10 (turn). Josh. 22:5 (serve); 23:14 (know). Judg. 10:16 (grieved); 16:16 (vexed). 1 Sam. 1:10 (bitterness of), 15 (poured out); 18:1 (knit with), 1 (loved as); 20:4 (desireth); 23:20 (desire); 30:6 (grieved). 2 Sam. 5:8 (hated). 1 Kings 2:4 (walk); 8:48 (return); 11:37 (desireth). 2 Kings 4:27 (vexed); 23:3 (keep), 25 (turned). 1 Chron. 22:19 (seek). 2 Chron. 6:38 (return); 15:12 (seek); 34:31 (keep). Job 3:20 (bitter); 7:11 (bitterness); 9:21 (know); 10:1 (weary), 1 (bitterness); 14:22 (mourn); 19:2 (vex); 21:25 (bitterness); 23:13 (desireth); 24:12 (wounded); 27:2 (vexed); 30:16 (poured out), 25 (grieved). Ps. 6:3 (sore vexed); 11:5 (hateth); 13:2 (take counsel); 19:7 (converting); 24:4 (not lifted up); 25:1 (lift up), 13 (dwell at ease); 31:7 (in adversities), 9 (consumed with grief); 33:20 (waiteth); 34:2 (boast); 35:9 (be joyful); 42:1 (panteth), 2 (thirsteth), 4 (pour out), 5 (cast down), 6 (cast down), 11 (cast down); 43:5 (cast down); 44:25 (bowed down); 49:18 (blessed); 57:1 (trusteth), 6 (bowed down); 62:1 (waiteth), 5 (wait); 63:1 (thirsteth), 5 (satisfied), 8 (followeth hard); 69:10 (chastened); 77:2 (refused to be comforted); 84:2 (longeth); 86:4 (rejoice), 4 (lift up); 88:3 (full of troubles); 94:19 (delight); 103:1, 2, 22; 104:1, 35 (bless); 107:5 (fainted), 9 (satisfieth), 9 (filleth with goodness), 26 (melted); 116:7 (return to rest); 119:20 (longing), 25 (cleaveth unto the dust), 28 (melteth for heaviness), 81 (fainteth), 129 (keep), 167 (kept); 123:4 (filled with scorning); 130:5 (wait), 6 (waiteth); 131:2 (quieted); 138:3 (strengthenedst); 139:14 (knoweth); 143:6 (thirsteth), 8 (lift up), 11 (bring out of trouble), 12 (afflict); 146:1 (praise). Prov. 2:10 (knowledge is pleasant); 3:22 (be life to); 13:4 (desireth), 4 (made fat), 19 (sweet to); 16:24 (sweet to); 19:2 (without knowledge), 18 (spare); 21:10 (desireth); 22:25 (get a snare to); 24:14 (wisdom unto); 25:13 (refresheth); 29:17 (give delight). Eccl. 2:24 (enjoy good); 6:3 (not filled); 7:28 (seeketh). Song 1:7; 3:1, 2, 3, 4 (loveth); 5:6 (failed); 6:12 (made me like chariots). Isa. 1:14 (hateth); 26:8 (desire), 9 (desired); 32:6 (make empty); 38:15 (bitterness of); 42:1 (delighteth); 55:2 (delight); 58:10 (draw out), 10 (afflicted), 11 (satisfy); 61:10 (joyful); 66:3 (delighteth). Jer. 4:31 (wearied); 5:9, 29 (avenged); 12:7 (dearly beloved of); 13:17 (shall weep); 14:19 (lothed); 31:12 (watered), 14 (satiate), 25 (satiated), 25 (sorrowful); 32:41 (whole); 50:19 (satisfied). Lam. 3:17 (removed), 20 (humbled), 24 (saith). Ezek. 7:19 (satisfy); 24:21 (pitieth). Jonah 2:7 (fainted). Hab. 2:4 (not upright). Zech. 11:8 (lothed), 8 (abhorred).

2. *mind(s)*—Gen. 23:8 (your). Deut. 18:6 (desire); 28:65 (sorrow). 1 Sam. 2:35 (mind). 2 Sam 17:8 (chafed). 2 Kings 9:15 (mind). 1 Chron. 28:9 (willing). Ezek. 23:17, 18, 22, 28 (alienated); 24:25 (set); 36:5 (despiteful).

3. *hearts*—Ex. 23:9 (heart). Lev. 26:16 (heart). Deut. 24:15 (heart). 1 Sam. 2:33 (grieve). 2 Sam. 3:21 (desireth). Ps. 10:3 (desire). Prov. 23:7 (heart); 28:25 (proud heart); 31:6 (heavy hearts). Jer. 42:20 (dissembled). Lam. 3:51 (affecteth). Ezek. 25:6 (rejoiced), 15 (despiteful); 27:31 (bitterness). Hos. 4:8 (set).

4. *hearty*—Prov. 27:9 (counsel).

5. *will*—Deut. 21:14 (she will). Ps. 27:12; 41:2. Ezek. 16:27.

6. *desire*—Eccl. 6:9. Jer. 22:27; 44:14. Mic. 7:3. Hab. 2:5.

7. *pleasure*—Ps. 105:22. Jer. 34:16.
8. *lust*—Ex. 15:9.
9. *angry*—Judg. 18:25.
10. *discontented*—1 Sam. 22:2.
11. *thyself*—Esther 4:13.
12. *myself*—Ps. 131:2.
13. *he*—Prov. 16:26.
14. *his own*—Prov. 14:10.
15. *Him*—Prov. 6:16.
16. *himself*—Jonah 4:8.
17. *herself*—Isa. 5:14.
18. *yourselves*—Jer. 37:9.
19. *man*—Isa. 49:7.
20. *so would we have it*—Ps. 35:25.

V. *Nephesh* is used of *man* 1. as a being "cut off" by God; 2. as a being slain or killed by man in 54 passages and is rendered in eight different ways:

1. Soul(s) cut off by God in 22 passages and rendered *soul(s)*:
   Gen. 17:14. Ex. 12:15, 19; 31:14. Lev. 7:20, 21, 25, 27; 17:10; 18:29; 19:8; 20:6; 22:3; 23:29, 30. Num. 9:13; 15:30, 31; 19:13, 20. Ezek. 18;4, 20.

2. Slain or killed by man in 31 passages, rendered in eight different ways:
   (a) *soul(s)*—Josh. 10:28, 30, 32, 35, 37 (twice), 39; 11:11. Ps. 59:3. Jer. 2:34. Ezek. 13:19; 22:25, 27.
   (b) *person(s)*—Deut. 27:25. Josh. 20:3, 9. 1 Sam. 22: 22. Prov. 28:17. Ezek. 17:17.
   (c) *any*—Lev. 24:17.
   (d) *any person*—Num. 31:19; 35:11, 15, 30 (twice). Ezek. 33:6.
   (e) *him*—Gen. 37:21. Deut. 19:6; 22:26.
   (f) *mortally*—Deut. 19:11.
   (g) *deadly*—Ps. 17:9.
   (h) *life*—2 Sam. 14:7.
   (i) *thee*—Jer. 40:14, 15.

VI. *Nephesh* is used of *man* as being mortal, subject to death of various kinds, from which he can be saved and delivered and life prolonged in 243 passages rendered in eleven different ways:

1. *soul(s)*—Gen. 12:13; 19:20; 35:18. Ex. 30:12, 15, 16. Lev. 17:11 (twice). Num. 16:38; 31:50. 1 Sam. 24:11; 25:29 (three times); 26:21. 2 Sam. 4:9. 1 Kings 1:29; 17:21, 22. Job 7:15; 27:8. Ps. 3:2; 6:4; 7:2, 5; 11:1; 17:13; 22:20, 29; 23:3; 25:20; 26:9; 33:19; 34:22; 35:3, 4, 12, 17; 40:14; 41:4; 49:8, 15; 54:3, 4; 55:18; 56:6, 13; 57:4; 59:3; 63:9; 66:9, 16; 69:1, 18; 70:2; 71:10, 13, 23; 72:13, 14; 74:19; 78:50; 86:2, 14; 88:14; 94:21; 97:10; 106:15; 109:20, 31; 116:4, 8; 119:109, 175; 120:2; 121:7; 124:4, 5, 7; 141:8; 142:4, 7; 143:3. Prov. 18:7; 24:12; 29:10. Isa. 3:9; 10:18; 44:20; 53:10, 11, 12; 55:3. Jer. 4:10; 20:13; 26:19; 38:17, 20; 44:7; 51:6, 45. Lam. 1:11, 16, 19; 2:12; 3:58. Ezek. 3:19, 21; 14:14, 20; 18:27; 33:5, 9. Hos. 9:4. Jonah 2:5. Hab. 2:10.

2. *life, lives*—Gen. 9:5 (twice); 19:17, 19; 32:30; 44:30 (twice). Ex. 4:19; 21:23 (twice), 30. Num. 35:31. Deut. 19:21 (twice); 24:6. Josh. 2:13, 14; 9:24. Judg. 5:18; 9:17; 12:3; 18:25 (twice). Ruth 4:15. 1 Sam. 19:5, 11; 20:1; 22:23 (twice); 23:15; 26:24 (twice); 28:9, 21; 2 Sam. 1:9; 4:8; 16:11; 18:13; 19:5; 23:17. 1 Kings 1:12 (twice); 2:23; 3:11; 19:2 (twice), 3, 4, 10, 14; 20:31, 39 (twice), 42 (twice). 2 Kings 1:13 (twice), 14; 7:7; 10:24 (twice). 1 Chron. 11:19 (twice). 2 Chron. 1:11. Esther 7:3, 7; 8:11; 9:16. Job 2:4, 6; 6:11; 13:14; 31:39. Ps. 31:13; 38:12. Prov. 1:18, 19; 6:26; 7:23; 13:3, 8. Isa. 15:4; 43:4. Jer. 4:30; 11:21; 19:7, 9; 21:7, 9; 22:25; 34:20, 21; 38:2, 16; 39:18; 44:30 (twice); 45:5; 46:26; 48:6; 49:37. Lam. 2:19; 5:9. Ezek. 32:10. Jonah 1:14; 4:3.

3. *give up the ghost* (i.e., die)—Job 11:20. Jer. 15:9.

4. *person*—2 Sam. 14:14.

5. *tablets* (Heb. literally, "houses of the soul," meaning bottles of essence [of perfume])—Isa. 3:20.

6. *deadly* (Heb. literally "enemies against my soul")—Ps. 17:9.
7. *himself*—1 Kings 19:4. Amos 2:14, 15.
8. *me*—Num. 23:10. Judg. 16:30. 1 Kings 20:32.
9. *they*—Job 36:14.
10. *themselves*—Isa. 47:14.
11. *yourselves*—Deut. 4:15. Josh. 23:11.

VII. *Nephesh* is used of man as actually dead in thirteen passages and is rendered in three different ways:
1. *the dead*—Lev. 19:28; 21:1; 22:4. Num. 5:2; 6:11.
2. *[dead] body*—Num. 9:6, 7, 10.
3. *dead body*—Lev. 21:11. Num. 6:6; 19:11, 13. Hag. 2:13.

VIII. *Nephesh* in thirteen passages (all rendered *soul*) is spoken of as going into a place described by four different words, translated as shown below:
1. *sheol* = the grave or gravedom. In five different passages it is rendered in two different ways:
   a. *grave*—Ps. 30:3; 89:48.
   b. *hell*—Ps. 16:10; 86:13. Prov. 23:14.
2. *shachath*—a pit for capturing wild beasts, hence, a grave. It occurs in six passages and is rendered in two different ways:
   a. *pit*—Job 33:18, 28, 30. Ps. 35:7. Isa. 38:17.
   b. *grave*—Job 33:22.
3. *shuchah*—a deep pit. It occurs in one passage only:
   a. *pit*—Jer. 18:20.
4. *dumah*—silence. It occurs in one passage only:
   a. *silence*—Ps. 94:17.

IX. *Nephesh* is used of the lower animals and man in seven passages and is rendered in three different ways:
1. *creature*—Gen. 9:15, 16.
2. *the life*—Lev. 17:11, 14 (three times).
3. *soul*—Num. 31:28.

X. *Nephesh* is used of the lower animals only in twenty passages and is rendered in nine different ways:
1. *creature*—Gen. 1:21, 24; 2:19; 9:10, 12. Lev. 11:46 (twice).

2. *thing*—Lev. 11:10. Ezek. 47:9.
3. *life*—Gen. 1:20, 30.
4. *the life*—Gen. 9:4. Deut 12:23 (twice). Prov. 12:10.
5. *beast*—Lev. 24:18 (three times).
6. *the soul*—Job 12:10.
7. *breath*—Job 41:21.
8. *fish*—Isa. 19:10.
9. *her*—Jer. 2:24.

Psuche

I. *Psuche* is used of man as an individual fourteen times and is rendered:

    1. *souls*—Acts 2:41, 43; 3:23; 7:14; 27:37. Rom. 2:9; 13:1. 1 Cor. 15:45. James 5:20. 1 Pet. 3:20. 2 Pet. 2:14. Rev. 6:9; 18:13; 20:4.

II. *Psuche* is used of the life of man, which can be lost, destroyed, saved, laid down, etc. As such it occurs fifty--eight times and is rendered:

    1. *life*—Matt. 2:20; 6:25 (twice); 10:39 (twice); 16:25 (twice); 20:28. Mark 3:4; 8:35 (twice); 10:45. Luke 6:9; 9:24 (twice), 56; 12:22, 23; 14:26; 17:33. John 10:11, 15, 17; 12:25 (twice); 13:37, 38; 15:13. Acts 15:26; 20:10, 24; 27:10, 22. Rom. 11:3; 16:4. Phil. 2:30. 1 John 3:16 (twice). Rev. 12:11.

    2. *souls*—Matt. 10:28 (twice); 16:26 (twice). Mark 8:36, 37. Luke 12:20; 21:19. 1 Thess. 2:8; 5:23. Heb. 4:12; 6:19; 10:39; 13:17. James 1:21. 1 Pet. 1:9; 2:11, 25; 4:19.

III. *Psuche* is used to emphasize the pronoun, the same as we use *self* in *myself*. It occurs in this sense twenty-one times and is rendered:

    1. *soul*—Matt. 11:29; 12:18; 26:38. Mark 14:34. Luke 1:46; 12:19 (twice). John 12:27. Acts 2:27, 31; 14:22; 15:24. 2 Cor. 1:23. Heb. 10:38. 1 Pet. 1:22. 2 Pet. 2:8. Rev. 18:14.

    2. *mind*—Acts 14:2. Heb. 12:3.

    3. *us*—John 10:24.

    4. *you*—2 Cor. 12:15.

IV. *Psuche* is used with intensive force to express all the powers of one's being. As such it occurs ten times and is rendered:

    1. *soul*—Matt. 22:37. Mark 12:30, 33. Luke 2:35; 10:27. Acts 4:32. 3 John 2.

    2. *heart*—Eph. 6:6.

    3. *mind*—Phil. 1:27.

    4. *heartily*—Col. 3:23.

V. *Psuche* is used of the lower animals twice and is rendered:

    1. *life*—Rev. 8:9.

    2. *soul*—Rev. 16:3.

Appendix B

Ruach

I. *Ruach* is used to mean wind, wind coming from one of the points of the compass, a point of the compass, invisible atmosphic conditions, and mere breath:

    1. *wind*—Gen. 8:1. Ex. 10:13, 19; 14:21; 15:10. Num. 11:31. 2 Sam. 22:11. 1 King 18:45; 19:11 (twice); 2 Kings 3:17. Job 1:19; 6:26; 7:7; 8:2; 15:2; 21:18; 28:25; 30:15, 22; 37:21. Ps. 1:4; 18:10, 42; 35:5; 48:7; 78:39; 83:13; 103:16; 104:3; 107:25; 135:7; 147:18; 148:8. Prov. 11:29; 25:14, 23; 27:16; 30:4. Eccl. 1:6; 5:16; 11:4. Isa. 7:2; 11:15; 17:13; 26:18; 27:8; 32:2; 41:16, 29; 57:13; 64:6. Jer. 2:24; 4:11, 12; 5:13; 10:13; 13:24; 14:6; 18:17; 22:22; 49:32, 36 (twice); 51:1, 16. Eze. 5:2, 10, 12; 12:14; 13:11, 13; 17:10, 21; 19:12; 27:26; 37:9 (twice). Dan. 2:35; 7:2; 8:8; 11:4. Hos. 4:19; 8:7; 12:1; 13:15. Amos 4:13. Jonah 1:4; 4:8. Zech. 2:6; 5:9.

    2. *quarters* (of the four winds)—1 Chron. 9:24.

    3. *sides* (of the four winds)—Jer. 52:23. Eze. 42:16,

17, 18, 19, 20.
4. *whirlwind*—Eze. 1:4.
5. *windy*—Ps. 55:8.
6. *spirits*—Zech. 6:5.
7. *air*—Job 41:16.
8. *tempest*—Ps. 11:6.
9. *blast*—Ex. 15:8. 2 Kings 19:7. Isa. 25:4; 37:7.
10. *breath*—Job 19:17

II. *Ruach* is used to mean the life-principle present in all living things, and breath or wind as the sign of the presence of the life-principle:
1. *spirit*—Num. 16:22; 27:16. Job 10:12; 27:3; 34:14. Ps. 31:5; 104:30. Eccl. 3:21 (twice); 8:8 (twice); 11:5; 12:7. Isa. 42:5. Eze. 37:14. Zech. 12:1.
2. *breath*—Gen. 6:17; 7:15, 22. Job 9:18; 12:10; 17:1. Ps. 104:29; 135:17; 146:4. Eccl. 3:19. Isa. 33:11; 42:5; Jer. 10:14; 51:17. Lam. 4:20. Eze. 37:5, 6, 8, 9, 10. Hab. 2:19.
3. *wind*—Eze. 37:9 (twice), 14.

III. *Ruach* is used in reference to Holy Spirit:
1. Gen. 1:2; 6:3. Num. 24:2. 1 Sam. 10:6, 10; 16:13; 19:20, 23. 2 Sam. 23:2. 1 Kings 18:12; 22:24. 2 Kings 2:16. 1 Chron. 12:18; 28:12. 2 Chron. 15:1; 18:23; 20:14; 24:20. Neh. 9:20, 30. Job 26:13; 33:4. Ps. 51:11, 12; 139:7; 143:10. Isa. 30:1; 34:16; 40:13; 48:16; 59:19, 21; 61:1; 63:10, 11, 14. Eze.1:12, 20 (three times), 21; 2:2; 3:12, 14, 24; 8:3; 10:17; 11:1, 5, 24; 37:1, 14; 43:5. Micah 2:7; 3:8. Hag. 2:5. Zech. 4:6; 6:8; 7:12. Mal. 2:15

IV. *Ruach* is used with reference to divine power manifesting itself in spiritual gifts:
1. *Spirit* or *spirit*—Gen. 41:38. Ex. 28:3; 31:3; 35:31. Num. 11:17, 25 (twice), 26, 29; 27:18. Deut. 34:9. Judges 3:10; 6:34; 11:29; 13:25; 14:6, 19; 15:14. 1 Sam. 11:6. 2 Kings 2:9, 15. 1 Chron. 12:18. Prov. 1:23. Isa. 11:2 (four times); 32:15; 42:1; 44:3; 59:21; 63:11. Eze. 11:19; 36:27;

39:29. Dan. 4:8, 9, 18; 5:11, 12, 14. Joel 2:28, 29. Zech. 12:10.

V. *Ruach* is used with reference to the invisible power of God, especially in executing judgment:
1. *blast*—Ex. 15:8. 2 Kings 19:7. Isa. 37:7.
2. *breath*—2 Sam. 22:16. Job 4:9; 15:30. Ps. 18:15; 33:6. Isa. 11:4; 30:28.
3. *spirit*—Isa. 4:4 (twice); 28:6; 40:7.

VI. *Ruach* is used to mean angelic beings both good and bad:
1. *angels*—Ps. 104:4.
2. *spirit*—Job 4:15. Isa. 31:3.
3. *evil spirit*—Judges 9:23. 1 Sam. 16:14, 15, 16, 23 (twice); 18:10; 19:9. 1 Kings 22:21, 22, 23. 2 Chron. 18:20, 21, 22.
4. *unclean spirit*—Zech. 13:2.

VII. *Ruach* is used to refer to the whole person:
1. *spirit*—Ps. 106:33. Prov. 11:13. Mal. 2:15, 16.

VIII. *Ruach* is used to refer to the mind as the invisible motivator of human activity, especially the emotions and the conscience:
1. *mind*—Gen. 26:35. Prov. 29:11. Eze. 11:5; 20:32. Dan. 5:20. Hab. 1:11.
2. *spirit*—Gen. 41:8; 45:27. Ex. 6:9; 35:21. Num. 5:14 (twice), 30; 14:24. Josh. 5:1. Judges 15:19. 1 Sam. 1:15; 30:12. 1 Kings 10:5; 21:5. 1 Chron. 5:26 (twice). 2 Chron. 9:4; 21:16; 36:22. Ezra 1:1, 5. Job 6:4; 7:11; 15:13; 20:3; 21:4; 32:8, 18. Ps. 32:2; 34:18; 51:10, 17; 76:12; 77:3, 6; 78:8; 142:3; 143:4, 7. Prov. 14: 29; 15:4, 13; 16:2, 18, 19, 32; 17:22, 27; 18:14 (twice); 5:28; 29:23. Eccl. 1:14, 17; 2:11, 17, 26; 4:4, 6, 16; 6:9; 7:8 (twice), 9; 10:4. Isa. 19:3, 14; 26:9; 29:10, 24; 38:16; 54:6; 57:15 (twice), 16; 61:3; 65:14; 66:2. Jer. 51:11. Eze. 13:3. Dan. 7:15. Hosea 4:12; 5:4. Micah 2:11.
3. *courage*—Josh. 2:11.
4. *anger*—Judges 8:3.

Pneuma

I. *Pneuma* is used with reference to God:
    1. *spirit*—John 4:24.

II. *Pneuma* is used with reference to Christ:
    1. *spirit*—1 Cor. 15:45. 2 Cor. 3:17, 18. Phil. 1:19. 1Pet. 1:11.

III. *Pneuma* is used with reference to the third person of the Godhead, who operates as an invisible Person or force:
    1. *Spirit* or *spirit*—Matt. 3:16; 4:1; 10:20; 12:18, 28. Mark 1:10, 12. Luke 2:27; 4:1, 14, 18; 11:13. John 1:32, 33; 3:5, 6, 8, 34; 7:39; 14:17; 15:26; 16:13. Acts 2:4, 17, 18; 5:9; 8:29, 39; 10:19; 11:12, 28; 16:7; 21:4. Rom. 1:4; 8:9 (twice); 8:13, 14, 16, 23, 26 (twice), 27; 15:19, 30. 1 Cor. 2:4, 10, 11 (twice), 14; 3:16; 6:11; 7:40; 12:3, 4, 7, 8 (twice), 9 (twice), 10, 11, 13 (twice). 2 Cor. 1:22; 3:3, 6; 5:5. Gal. 3:2, 3, 5, 14; 4:6; 5:18, 22, 25 (twice). Eph. 1:13; 2:18, 22; 3:5, 16; 4:3, 4, 30; 5:9, 18; 6:17. Phil. 2:1. 2 Thess. 2:13. 1 Tim. 3:16; 4:1. 1 Pet. 1:22; 3:18. 1 John 4:2, 6, 13, 14. Jude 19. Rev. 1:4; 2:7, 11, 17, 29; 3:1, 6, 13, 22; 4:5; 5:6; 14:13; 22:17.

    2. *Holy Ghost* (another translation for Holy Spirit: Matt. 1:18, 20; 3:11; 12:32; 28:19. Mark 1:8; 3:29; 12:36; 13:11. Luke 1:15, 35, 41, 67; 2:25, 26; 3:16, 22; 4:1; 12:10, 12. John 1:33; 7:39; 14:26; 20:22. Acts 1:2, 5, 8, 16; 2:4, 33, 38; 4:8, 31; 5:3, 32; 6:3, 5; 7:51, 55; 8:15, 17, 18, 19; 9:17, 31; 10:38, 44, 45, 47; 11:15, 16, 24; 13:2, 4, 9, 52; 15:8, 28; 16:6; 19:2 (twice), 6; 20:23, 28; 21:11; 28:25. Rom. 5:5; 9:1; 14:17; 15:13, 16. 1 Cor. 2:13; 6:19; 12:3. 2 Cor. 6:6; 13:14. 1 Thess. 1:5, 6. 2 Tim. 1:14. Titus 3:5. Heb. 2:4; 3:7; 6:4; 9:8; 10:15. 1 Pet. 1:12. 2 Pet. 1:21. 1 John 5:7. Jude 20.

IV. *Pneuma* is used to mean an actuating principle:
    1. 1 Cor. 2:12; 6:17. 2 Cor. 3:8; 4:13; 11:4; 12:18. Gal. 5:17; 6:1, 8. Eph. 2:2; 4:23. Phil. 1:27. 2 Thess. 2:8. Heb. 9:14; 10:29. James 4:5. 1 Pet. 4: 14.

1 John 3:24. Rev. 1:10; 4:2; 17:3; 19:10; 21:10.

V. *Pneuma* is used to mean mind or character or conscience:
1. *spirit*—Matt. 5:3; 26:41. Mark 2:8; 8:12; 14:38. Luke 1:17, 80; 2:40; 9:55; 10:21. John 11:33; 13:21. Acts 6:10; 17:16; 18:5, 25; 19:21; 20:22. Rom. 8:15 (twice), 16; 11:8. 1 Cor. 4:21; 5:4; 7:34; 14:14, 15 (twice). 2 Cor. 2:13; 7:1. Eph. 1:17. 1 Thess. 4:8; 5:19. 1 Tim. 4:12. 2 Tim. 1:7. 1 Pet. 1:2; 3:4, 19.

VI. *Pneuma* may be rendered by a possessive pronominal adjective, such as my, your, or his, modifying spirit:
1. Luke 1:47. 1 Cor. 16:18. 2 Cor. 7:13. Gal. 6:18. 2 Tim. 4:22. Philemon 25.

VII. *Pneuma,* translated *spirit* is used to mean a born-again individual:
1. John 3:6. 1 Cor. 5:5. Heb. 12:9, 23.

VIII. *Pneuma* is translated various ways to mean spiritual gift:
1. Matt. 22:43. Rom. 8:2. 2 Thess. 2:2.

IX. *Pneuma* is used to mean spiritually:
1. *in (the, my, your, etc.) spirit*—John 4:23, 24. Rom. 12:11. 1 Cor. 5:3; 6:20; 14:2. Gal. 5:16. Eph. 6:18. Phil. 3:3. Col. 2:5. 1 Pet. 4:6. Rev. 1:10; 17:3.
2. *with (the, my, your) spirit*—Rom. 1:9; 2:29; 7:6. 1 Cor. 14:15 (twice); 16. Gal. 3:3; 4:29.
3. *after the (my, your) spirit*—Rom. 8:4, 5, 9. Gal. 4:29.
4. *through . . . the spirit*—1 Pet. 1:2.

X. *Pneuma* is used to mean either the physical or spiritual life principle:
1. *spirit*—Luke 8:55; 23:46. John 6:63 (twice). Acts 7:59. Rom. 8:10, 11, 13. 1 Cor. 15:45. 2 Cor. 3:6. Gal. 6:8. Col. 1:8. 1 Thess. 5:23. Heb. 4:12. James 2:26. Rev. 11:11.
2. *yielded or gave up the ghost* (i.e., expired)— Matt. 27:50. John 19:30.
3. *life*—Rev. 13:15.

XI. *Pneuma* is used to mean wind, an invisible agent:
1. *spirit*—John 3:8.

XII. *Pneuma* us used to refer to a spirit entity:
>   1. *spirit*—Luke 24:37, 39. Acts 23:8, 9. Heb. 1:14.
>   1 John 4:1 (twice), 2, 3.

XIII. *Pneuma* is used to mean good angels:
>   1. *spirits*—Heb. 1:7.

XIV. *Pneuma* is used to mean evil angels:
>   1. Matt. 8:16; 10:1; 12:43, 45. Mark 1:23, 26, 27;
>   3:11, 30; 5:2, 8, 13; 6:7; 7:25; 9:17, 20, 25 (twice).
>   Luke 4:33, 36. 6:18; 7:21; 8:2, 29; 9:39, 42;
>   10:20; 11:24, 26; 13:11. Acts 5:16; 8:7; 16:16, 18;
>   19:12, 13, 15, 16. 1 Tim. 4:1. Rev. 16:13, 14;
>   18:2.

Appendix C

Neshamah

I. *Neshamah* is used to mean simply breath, or breath as
the sign or presence of the life-principle:
>   1. *breath*—Gen. 2:7; 7:22. 1 Kings 17:17. Job 33:4;
>   34:14; 37:10. Ps. 150:6. Isa. 2:22; 30:33; 42:5.
>   Dan. 5:23; 10:17.
>   2. *inspiration* (i.e., breath)—Job 32:8
>   3. *that breatheth* (Heb. literally, that hath breath)—
>   Deut. 20:16.
>   4. *that breathed* (Heb. literally, that had breath)—
>   Josh. 10:40. 1 Kings 15:29.
>   5. *to breathe* (Heb. literally, to have breath)—Josh.
>   11:11, 14.
>   6. *blast*—2 Sam. 22:16. Job 4:9. Ps. 18:15.
>   7. *spirit*—Job 27:3. Prov. 20:27 (probably meaning
>   consciousness or conscience).
>   8. *souls*—Isa. 57:16.

Appendix D

Unconsciousness in Death

Job 7:21; 14:10-12, 21; Ps. 39:13; 88:10-12; 146:2-4; Eccl. 9:5, 6, 10.

Appendix E

Resurrection Theme

1 Sam. 2:6; Job 19:25-27; Ps. 16:9, 10; Isa. 26:19; Eze. 37:13; Dan. 12:2; Luke 14:14; John 5:28, 29; 6:39, 40, 44, 54; 11:24,; Acts 4:2; 17:18; 23:6; 24:15; Rom. 8:23; 1 Cor. 15:12-23, 35-44, 49-55. 1 Thess. 4:16; 1 Pet. 1:3; Rev. 20:6.

References

Chapter 1

1. Raymond Moody, *Life After Life* (Atlanta: Mockingbird Books, 1977), pp. 23, 24.
2. From OUT ON A LIMB, by Shirley MacLaine, p. 179. Copyright © 1983 by Shirley MacLaine. Reprinted by permission of Bantam Books. All rights reserved.

Chapter 2

1. "Scientists probe the unexplainable," *Idaho Press-Tribune* (Caldwell-Nampa), August 9, 1987, section A, p. 1.
2. David F. Marks, "Investigating the Paranormal," *Nature,* vol. 320, no. 13, March 1986, pp. 119-124.
3. Emma Hardinge Britten, *Nineteenth Century Miracles* (New York: published by William Britten, printed by Lovell & Co., 1884), p. 555.
4. Archie Matson, *Afterlife: Reports From the Threshold of Death* (New York: Harper & Row, Publishers, 1975), p. 67.
5. Arthur Conan Doyle, *The New Revelation* (New York: Hodder and Stoughton, 1918), pp. 123, 124.
6. George E. Vandeman, *Psychic Roulette* (New York: Thomas Nelson Inc., 1973), p. 32.
7. *Encyclopedia of Occultism & Parapsychology*, Leslie Shepard, ed. (Detroit, Mich.: Gale Research Company, 1978), S. V. "Communication."

Chapter 3

1. "Seven Lost Years," *Time*, December 26, 1955, pp. 33, 34.

Chapter 4

1. Glen O. Gabbard, Stuart W. Twemlow, and Fowler C. Jones, "Do 'Near Death Experiences' Occur Only Near Death?" *The Journal of Nervous and Mental Disease*, vol. 169, no. 6 (June 1981), p. 374.

2. Arthur Bateman, *Christianity and Spiritualism* (London: The Epworth Press, 1923), pp. 15, 16.

3. Matson, p. 78.

4. David H. Lund, *Death and Consciousness* (Jefferson, N.C.: McFarland & Company, Inc., Publishers, 1985), pp. 5, 6.

5. John Kobler, "The Dangerous Magic of LSD," *Saturday Evening Post*, vol. 236 (Nov. 2, 1963), pp. 31, 32.

6. Aldous Huxley, *The Doors of Perception* (New York: Harper and Brothers, 1956), p. 52.

7. Sanford M. Unger, "Mescaline, LSD, Psilocybin and Personality Change," *Psychiatry*, vol. 26 (May 1963), p. 113. Footnote states that the quotation was translated from a subject's account in K. Beringer, *Der Meskalinrausch* (Berlin: Springer, 1927); and quoted in Robert S. DeRopp, *Drugs and the Mind* (New York: Grove, 1957), p. 51.

8. L. J. Meduna, ed., *Carbon Dioxide Therapy* (Springfield, Ill.: Charles C. Thomas, Publisher, 1950), p. 23.

9. *Ibid.*, p. 28.

10. Melvin Morse, et. al., "Childhood Near-Death Experiences," *The American Journal of Diseases of Children*, vol. 140 (November 1986), pp. 1112, 1113.

11. Ian Stevenson and Bruce Greyson, "Near-Death Experiences: Relevance to the Question of Survival After Death," *Journal of the American Medical Association*, vol. 242, no. 3 (July 20, 1979), p. 266.

12. Satwant Pasricha and Ian Stevenson, "Near-Death Experiences in India: A Preliminary Report," *The Journal of Nervous and Mental Disease*, vol. 174, no. 3 (March 1986), p. 170.

92 THE MYSTERY OF CONSCIOUSNESS

13. Russell Noyes; et. al., *The Journal of Nervous and Mental Disease*, vol. 164, no. 6, p. 401.

14. From *Teach Only Love*, as quoted in *Orange County Resources*, "Interview with Gerald Jampolsky, M.D.," by Phil Friedmann, Ph. D., p. 3. Cited in *The Seduction of Christianity*, by Dave Hunt and T. A. McMahon (Eugene, Ore.: Harvest House Publishers, 1985), p. 58.

15. *Handbook of Parapsychology*, Benjamin B. Wolman, ed. (San Francisco: Van Nostrand Reinhold Company, 1977), p. 608.

16. Michael B. Sabom, "The Near-Death Experience," Letter to the editor of *Journal of the American Medical Association*, vol. 244, no. 1 (July 4, 1980), p. 29.

Chapter 5

1. "Dead Man Revived and Kept Alive Several Hours by Modern Miracle," *The Oregonian*, June 14, 1933, section A, pp. 1 and 3.

2. Philip Schaff, *The Creeds of Christendom, With a History and Critical Notes* (New York: Harper & Brothers, 1881), vol. 1, p. 21.

Chapter 6

1. David G. Myers, "ESP and the Paranormal: Supernatural or Super-fraud?" *Christianity Today*, vol. 27, no. 11 (July 15, 1983), p. 16.

2. "Appendixes to the Companion Bible," *The Companion Bible* (New York: Oxford University Press, nd.), "Ruach," p. 13; "Nephesh," p. 19; "Neshamah," p. 23; "Pneuma," p. 146; and "Psuche," p. 153.

Robert Young, *Analytical Concordance to the Bible* (New York: Funk & Wagnalls Company, nd.), "Index-lexicon to the Old Testament," "Nedibah," p. 31; "Nephesh," p. 31; "Neshamah," p. 32; "Ob," p. 32; "Ruach," p. 41. "Index-lexicon to the New Testament," "Phantasma," p. 84; "Pneuma," p. 86; "Psuche," p. 88.

The New Englishman's Hebrew Concordance, [George

V.] Wigram, sponsor (Peabody, Mass.: Hendrickson Publishers, Inc., 1984), p. 29, *ob*; pp. 829-833, *nephesh*; pp. 1160-1162, p. 849, *neshamah*; pp. 1160-1162 *ruach*.

The New Englishman's Greek Concordance and Lexicon, George V. Wigram, ed.; Jay P. Green, rev. ed. (Peabody, Mass.: Hendrickson Publishers, Inc., 1982), pp. 723-726, *pneuma*; pp. 929, 930, *psuche*.

3. J. I. Marais, "Psychology," *The International Standard Bible Encyclopedia* (Grand Rapids, Mich.: Wm. B. Eerdmans Publishing Company, 1939), vol. 4, p. 2495.

4. Alfred E. Garvie, "Soul," *Dictionary of the Bible* (New York: Charles Scribner's Sons, 1918), p. 872.

Chapter 7

1. Robert McAfee Brown, "Immortality," *A Handbook of Christian Theology* (New York: Meridian Books, Inc., 1958), p. 183.

Chapter 9

1. L. P. Jacks, "The Confessions of an Octogenarian," pp. 229, 230. Quoted by Francis D. Nichol in *Review and Herald*, June 28, 1956, p. 9.

2. Ralph L. Keiper, "The Resurrection and the Second Coming," *Eternity*, April 1955, p. 10.

Chapter 10

1. B. H. Carroll, "The Pastoral Epistles of Paul and I and II Peter, Jude and I, II, III John," *An Interpretation of the English Bibles* (Nashville, Tenn.: The Broadman Press, 1942), pp. 248-250.

2. Adam Clarke, *The Holy Bible, Containing the Old and New Testament . . . with a Commentary and Critical Notes* (New York: Carlton & Phillips, 1853, new ed., with the author's final corrections), vol. 6, p. 861.

Chapter 11

1. Kurt E. Koch, *Occult ABC* (Grand Rapids, Mich: Kregel Publications, enlarged and revised, 1986), pp. 223, 224.

2. *The Works of Flavius Josephus*, William Whiston, trans. (Grand Rapids, Mich.: Baker Book House, 1984), "Josephus's Discourse to the Greeks Concerning Hades," vol. 4, pp. 239-243.

Chapter 12

1. Charles M. Snow, *On the Throne of Sin* (Takoma Park, Md.: Review and Herald Publishing Association, 1927), pp. 104, 105. Quoted from the *African Sentinel* of September, 1921.

2. MacLaine, *Out on a Limb*, p. 209.

3. From IT'S ALL IN THE PLAYING, by Shirley MacLaine, pp. 256, 257. Copyright © 1987 by Shirley MacLaine. Reprinted by permission of Bantam Books. All rights reserved.

4. Dave Hunt and T. A. McMahon, *The Seduction of Christianity* (Eugene, Ore.: Harvest House Publishers, 1985), p. 52.

5. *Ibid.*, p. 56.

6. Harry Rimmer, *The Evidences for Immortality* (Nashville, Tenn.: Wm. B. Eerdmans Publishing Co., 1942, fourth ed.), pp. 42, 43.

Chapter 13

1. J. W. Daniels, *Spiritualism Versus Christianity; or, Spiritualism Thoroughly Exposed* (New York and Auburn: Miller, Orton & Mulligan, 1856), pp. 82-84.

DATE DUE

			PRINTED IN U.S.A.